Eddie's War

Eddie's War

CAROL FISHER SALLER

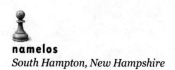

namelos
South Hampton, New Hampshire

Library of Congress Control Number: 2011925808

ISBN 978-1-60898-108-3 (hardcover : alk. paper)
ISBN 978-1-60898-109-0 (pbk. : alk. paper)
ISBN 978-1-60898-110-6 (ebk.)

namelos
www.namelos.com

In memory of my father, Kenneth Fisher

Contents

Paperboy

In town Thomas pulled me by the hand
through the books.
He found the short shelf
marked Children.
"Stay put," he said;
"I'm going to the barber,"
and he left.
I looked at the shelf,
then walked back
to the front of the library
to look again
at something I'd seen.
An old man
at a table near the window,
the man who sometimes tended our horse
if she seemed lame
or needed shoeing.
He squinted down through glasses
at big sheets of paper
he held up to the light.
He'd close the sheets together,
open them again,
rustle, snap, open, close,
like wings of a big, papery moth.
Miss Fenton, the librarian, saw me.
I knew her from church.
"Eddie Carl," she whispered,
"may I help you?"

I pointed.
Smiling, she walked to a rack of papers
draped over wooden bars.
"Let's see," she said,
still whispering.
"*St. Louis Post-Dispatch*
or *Peoria Star*?"
She nodded toward the old man.
"Mr. Mirga has the *Canton Ledger*."
St. Louis was foreign,
mysterious.
"*St. Louis* . . . what you said," I decided.
I turned the big pages,
sniffed the ink,
grown-up, important.
Soon I could read the headlines:
"Kills Sweetheart, Takes Body Home"
or "Liverpool Farmer Found Dead in Bed."
And the advertisements:
"Doan's Pills clean out kidney poisons:
Wash out your 15 miles of kidney tubes."
Or "Indulge in golf while a roast is cooking.
Set the Therm-O-Matic and all is safe."
You could learn just about anything
kneeling on a chair,
elbows on the paper,
at a yellow pine table at the public library
in Ellisville, Illinois.

The Foxes

When the *Hindenburg* caught fire
and fell out of the sky,
I saw the pictures
in the paper.
"I seen 'em, Tom," I was saying,
out south cutting thistles,
"people jumping out
an' it still up in the air"—
But Thomas looked up,
said hush.
There was whining
somewhere in the grass.
We followed the sounds.
On his knees Thomas dug with his hands
into the hill
into the den,
handed them out one by one,
little foxes.
Our shirttails held the kits,
four in all,
little, soft, wriggly.
"We better git
before their ma sees us," said Thomas.
We put them in the silo pit,
watched them lap milk
with their little tongues.
All that week between chores
we ran to the silo

to watch them tumble and play.
One I named Bitsy
liked me best.
She'd root around, snuffle my hands.
I'd put her up to my neck,
laughing,
her nose wet and poky.
Dad came, stood in the door.
"Time to get rid of 'em," he said,
"tomorrow."
"But—" I started, then stopped,
seeing the set of his jaw.
That night in our room Tom sat at the desk,
me on the bed.
"Dad's right," he said. "They're pests."
"I ain't doing it," I said.
"I'll do it," he said.
He was thirteen.
I got up and stomped out.
Next day, Bitsy in my lap,
I looked up, saw Thomas,
.22 in one hand,
gunnysack in the other.
"No," I pleaded. "Look how little—"
"Come on," he said,
gruff.
He scooped the kits into the bag,
headed out.
"Mom said you'd drown 'em," I said,
trotting behind.
"I'm not gonna drown 'em."

Thomas tramped on into the alfalfa
through the walnuts
into the pasture.
He stopped, set down the wriggling bag,
slid a cartridge into the rifle.
I didn't mean to watch,
but I did.
He fired once, twice, three times,
four,
into the air,
then reached down,
untied the sack.
The little foxes bumbled out,
blinking in the light,
then scampered away
toward the walnuts.
Bitsy never looked back.
Thomas watched them go,
squinted down at me.
I could hardly speak. "Dad said—"
"Dad's right," he said.
He put a hand on my head,
gave it a shake.
"But we're right, too."
I grabbed him around the waist,
held on tight.

July 1938
The Argument

"Eddie!" yelled Thomas. "Hammer!"
I sprinted for the shed.
Thomas and his friends
Gabe and Curtis Ray
were building a tree fort
in the oak by the pond.
Gabe had the claw hammer,
pulling nails out of boards.
Half a foot taller and thirty pounds up
on the others,
still he never told me
to bug off or scram.
"Hey, Gabe," I said,
"know what I read?"
"Naw, what?" he said,
yanking on a nail.
I squatted down beside him.
"I read about this guy
over t' Henry County,
busted a killer outta jail,
hung him from a tree."
Gabe kept at the nails.
"Ain't right," he said.
"But this killer,"
I said, "he woulda got hung anyways."
"Still ain't right."
"How come?" I asked.
Gabe frowned.

"Mighta been a mistake.
He might not a done it."
"Did, too! Everybody saw it."
That part wasn't in the newspaper.
"Okay," said Gabe,
"but there's laws."
He leaned on a board,
pointed the hammer at me.
"And why is it right
to kill the killer
but not right for him to
kill someone hisself?"
He went back to pulling nails.
I chewed on this a bit.
"Gabe," I said finally,
"how come you ain't so smart
in school?"
"Don't know," he answered. "Just ain't."

July 1938
The Tree Fort

Over that week
the fort took shape.
Thomas, up in the tree,
bounced on a branch, testing it.
"We'll put the floor here," he said.
He leaned out, pointing,
in charge.
"We'll tie the rope up there."

He'd got the idea one night,
tried it out in bed
in the dark,
whispering.
"We can hide out," he'd said.
"When the enemy comes
we'll swing on a rope,
drop into the pond."
I watched and fetched
as they hauled the floor up,
then a wall, then two,
till the only thing left
was to tie the swing rope.
"I'll do it," said Curtis Ray.
Scrawny and lithe,
he knew his way around a tree.
He got a foothold,
climbed past the floor
about eight feet up,
then another six to straddle the branch,
leaned forward,
inchwormed out.
"Toss 'er up!" he called.
Thomas, in the fort, threw,
the rope snaking up and out.
Curt swung an arm, wild,
and missed—
rolled off the branch,
caught hold for a second,
fell feet first,
but a foot hit the edge of the floor,

enough to tip him.
He landed hard, on his side.
Gabe and I stood frozen.
Thomas swung down.
Curtis Ray whimpered,
"Something's broke—something's broke!"
Thomas went down on one knee.
"Don't worry—" he said,
"we'll get you to the house.
We'll get the doctor."
He turned to Gabe and me.
"Get a board."
We put the board next to Curtis Ray,
shifted him on gently as we could,
him crying out,
swearing.
"Lift!" Thomas ordered.
But lifting rocked the board,
nearly tipped him into the dirt.
Curtis Ray turned pale as the birches,
eyes rolling up.
"Get back," said Gabe.
He bent forward on one knee,
shoved his arms under the board,
staggered to his feet.
He turned toward the house.
I ran ahead, yelling, "Mom! Dad!"
Thomas hung close to Gabe
in case he tired.
But Gabe kept on marching,
one foot

then the other,
like he wasn't even thinking,
just doing what he had to do.
When we got to the Ford
alongside the house
Thomas and I opened the doors,
helped Gabe slide Curtis Ray in.
Later it came back
Curt's hip was broken, bad—
enough to keep him out of trees
all summer.
Gabe—he was a hero,
got his name in the *Ellisville Baptist Chatter*,
but it didn't swell his head any.
He still never told me to bug off
or scram.

September 1938
Dad's Story

I lolled on the sofa,
bored.
Dad and Thomas cleaned their rifles,
sitting in armchairs, guns in pieces,
flannel dabbed with oil.
Thomas was fourteen.
I was nine.
"Dad," I said, flopping belly down
on the footstool,
"Do I got to wait till I'm eleven

like Thomas?"

"And why wouldn't you?" answered Dad,
not looking up.

"Well, I figure I had all this time
to watch you and Tom.
I probably know more than he did.
I'm readier."

"Yeah, well, that's what I thought
when I was about your age," he said,
"and you know what happened."

I grinned. "Yeah, I know.
Tell it again."

Dad laid the rifle across his lap,
one foot nudging me off the stool
to put his feet up,
and began.

Well, it was spring.
I was helping my pa mend the fence
around the milkhouse pen,
a wood fence back then, you know—
thirty cows shoving along it
day after day
and ever so often
the whole thing would sag.
Pa'd dig and fill and shore it up again.
It was my job
to hold the fence upright.
I stood there thinking,
waiting for the right time
to speak up.
We were near done

when I got up the nerve.
"Pa," I said,
"I think I could try that shotgun
again."
Pa kept digging,
didn't answer right away.
I went on. "I'm ten now
and a lot bigger
and I'm getting stronger all the time."
"That so?" Pa asked.
His mind seemed set
on tromping that soil down good.
"Sure," I said. "You did it
when you were nine."
Pa took out his hankie, mopped his brow.
"Right then—let's go."
I felt my stomach drop a couple inches
as we started toward the house.
At seven, I'd begged for a .22
and Pa told me the rule:
"When you can shoot my big ol' 12-gauge
and not land on your rump,
you'll be ready for a rifle."
I'd leaned against the old hickory,
shouldered the shotgun,
braced, fired—
and the kickback was so hard
I dropped the gun,
shoulder shooting pain
that turned into a bruise
the size of a cow pie,

blue, then gray,
then a sick sort of yellow.
So now we got the shotgun,
walked out behind the barn
to that same old hickory.
Pa cocked the gun, held it out.
I took my time,
my back against the tree,
hard,
jamming the butt in my armpit.
I raised the gun,
sighted along the barrel,
concentrated on holding tight,
squeezed the trigger.
I took the slam in my shoulder,
nearly lost hold
but tightened up in time.
I whooped
and turned to Pa—
but he didn't seem to notice.
He was looking down the meadow,
squinting past the fence
into the trees by the pond.
"Damn it, boy—!" he yelled.
Grabbing the gun,
he took off running.
"You're shootin' the damn sheep!"
Turned out
I'd only nicked the leg of a ewe,
lamed it a little,
but there sure weren't no .22 that time.

"If you was aimin' at the sheep
yer too dumb to have a gun," Pa said.
"And if you wasn't—well,
Lord help us when you get one."

September 1938
Duck Hunting

Hunkered in the duck blind,
watching,
trying to keep still,
broken reeds
poking through my jacket,
I squirmed.
Long fingers
like barn nails
gripped my neck:
Grampa Rob.

September 1938
Jozef Mirga

The day Jozef talked
was chilly and wet.
I tramped into the library
brushing muddy leaves
from my boots.
The old man was at the table.
He looked up

but quick looked down again.
The papers were on the table
so I squirmed out of my jacket
and settled in across from him.
He had the Peoria paper.
"Excuse me," I whispered,
"you done with the *Ledger*?"
He looked startled
and put down the *Star*.
"Ah," he said, "please."
He motioned over the table.
"And please, I am Jozef."
I nodded. "Yo-sef," I repeated,
saying it the way he had.
I picked up the *Ledger*
and Jozef picked up the *Star* again.
I liked to skip around,
looking for something short:
I was reading about a town in Missouri
with too many spiders
when Jozef made a gravelly noise
in his throat
so I looked up.
"You are small boy to read,"
he pointed out.
I shrugged.
"You are reading long time," he added.
I nodded.
He glanced around, leaned closer.
"You help this old man?"
I nodded.

Jozef reached inside his jacket,
pulled out a piece of paper
folded many times.
He worked it open,
long fingers fumbling.
The scrap looked old and thin.
He was careful not to tear it.
When the paper was open
he put it on the table,
poked a finger on it.
"Is my town," he said. "I look for news."
The scrap was upside down
so I reached out,
turned it around.
Jozef didn't take his eyes off it.
"You read," he said.
"Poland," I read,
and then strange words. "Nowy Targ?"
I guess he didn't really believe
I could read,
'cause he looked at me
like I'd eaten it
instead of just reading it.
"Ya," he said,
drawing it back toward himself.
"Nowy Targ is city in Polska.
Poland, you say."
I paused, pondering.
"Why would it be in the newspaper?"
I asked.
Jozef didn't answer

as he folded the paper
over and over,
put it away.
"I hope is not there," he said finally,
smoothing the front of his jacket.
He tapped the place on his chest
where the paper was.
"You are seeing the words in newspaper?
Please to tell me."
Even I knew this seemed
out and out unlikely.
But I nodded and promised.
"Yes, sir—
I will."

September 1938
Stinky Dawson

Stinky liked to talk
but he wasn't that great at
listening.
Sylvester Dean Dawson.
I'd known him so long
I couldn't remember when he got to be
Stinky—
probably something to do with diapers.
The Dawsons' farm was to the west,
a raggedy kind of place,
Fern and Dale and eleven kids,
Stinky in the middle,

hand-me-down, make do, do without—
that was the Dawsons.
Stinky scrabbled for pocket money,
tended the coal at church,
did chores for neighbors.
Liked to talk
even when he didn't know anything,
which was most of the time.
Not that he was a fibber, exactly,
but his mind was odd
the way it took stuff in
and messed it around.
He'd tell a tale
and the thing was,
crazy as it sounded,
you'd want to believe him.
Sometimes even I believed him.
Kids teased him
but we got along pretty well.
We were pals mostly 'cause
he'd lived all my life
a few hundred yards
past our pond.
The day I had new boots,
I crunched in the barnyard gravel
right through the puddles.
I wanted to show Stinky.
I ran toward the pond,
knowing it would be full
after the rain.
I saw him in the distance

and hollered,
"Stink-eeeeee!"
He looked up and waved back.
As I trotted up,
he was poking in the pond
with a stick.
"Something's there.
I'm trying to get it."
Barefoot,
he looked at my new boots.
"Why you got those on?" he asked.
I shrugged.
They were black, with shiny clasps,
like my dad's.
I found a good stick and we poked
together.
"Could be a box," I said,
"with money in it.
These guys in Granite City
found a thousand bucks
in an ash can.
It was in the newspaper."
Stinky looked interested.
"They had to give it back," I allowed.
Stinky went back to poking
but soon sighed.
"Why don't you wade in?" he said.
"Not me," I said. "Might be snakes."
"Then gimme your boots—
I'll do it."
I couldn't think of a better plan,

so I yanked off the boots,
and Stinky pulled them on.
Using both sticks to balance,
he put one foot forward,
then the other.
The water was green and scummy;
we couldn't see how deep it was.
After a few steps
Stinky tried to raise a foot
and nearly fell over.
He grunted, pulled harder,
and slowly started to sink,
sucked into the mud.
Water poured into the boots.
"I'm stuck!" he whimpered.
"Eddie!
I can't get out,
—and there might be snakes!"
I didn't know what to do.
I sure wasn't wading in.
"Should I get your mom?"
"No!"
"I thought you weren't afraid of snakes,"
I argued.
"I ain't," he insisted,
"I just don't like 'em."
"Well, me either!
So let me get your mom."
"Gol darn it, Eddie! I *am* afraid of snakes
and I'm afraid of my mom!"
He started sniveling. "You gotta help me!

They're gonna get me! They're gonna—"
But I was there,
squishing into the cool mud,
grabbing him around the waist,
pulling with all my might.
One foot popped up,
and as we both fell back with a murky splash,
the other foot came up, too.
Shrieking, we scrambled out,
leaving the boots behind.
We sat, dripping.
Stinky stopped crying.
I looked at the green scum
settling back in.
"We better get those boots,"
I said.
Stinky didn't answer.
I guessed he hadn't heard me.
"I lose those boots," I went on,
"I'm sure gonna get it."
Stinky threw the piece of grass he was chewing
into the scum.
"Well, don't look at me!" he said,
"I already saved you
from the snakes."

October 1938

The Gossips

"Edward Carl, don't dawdle."
Grama Lucy gripped my elbow
and lifted
till I was on the tips of my toes
as she hustled us down Main Street.
I wasn't dawdling,
just trying to read the headlines
of *Official Detective*
in the five-and-dime window.
"Who Left Leona in Lover's Lane?"
was all I saw
before Grama grabbed my elbow.
"Don't look at that trash," she said,
propelling me past.
Turning the corner,
we about smacked into
Effie Thompson
dragging Dulcie by the hand.
Effie spruce and orderly,
Dulcie like someone else's child,
hair in her eyes,
slip hanging down.
Grama said, "Pardon, Effie!"
and let go my elbow.
Effie frowned.
"Lucy Carl, look at your wrist!
Black and blue from
hen pecks.

You got to wear gloves
like me. Land sakes—
you look like a farm woman."
"Well, yes—I mean, I know."
Grama did wear gloves,
but I guess there wasn't much point
telling Effie.
Effie sniffed,
looked at her daughter
and sighed.
"We're buying shoes.
Way she runs down her heels—
looks like a gypsy."
They bustled away
and Grama plowed on.
"What's a gypsy?" I asked,
trotting along.
Grama considered. "You know—
them folks in the shacks
out toward Fiatt."
"Do we know any?" I asked.
"Sakes no!
Keep to themselves.
Don't go to church—
don't go to school.
Talk their own language.
Not like us."
"Do they farm?"
"They can't—
they don't own any ground!
One of them's a blacksmith—that fella Mirga—

but mostly they're just beggars
and thieves.
It's in their blood."
Jozef was a gypsy?
"Jozef ain't a beggar or thief."
Grama stopped,
took hold of my sleeve.
"Joseph Mirga?
What do you know about him?"
I squirmed.
"He shoes Hettie sometimes.
I see him at the library.
He just reads.
He doesn't steal nothing."
Grama sighed, marched on.
"You stay clear of that one.
Hmmph. The library!
That's ridiculous."
"Why?" I asked.
"Because," she hooted,
"them gypsies
don't know how to read!"

October 1938
Curtis Ray

When Curtis Ray's mother died
the funeral home was packed.
Annylee was young,
Curtis Ray only thirteen.

Everyone whispered—
What will Charles Darney do,
poor, overworked,
raising a boy on his own,
and that Curtis Ray
a handful.
"Friends," said Reverend James,
"we have lost a dear sister.
Why the Lord chose Annylee
we cannot know,
but now she is with the angels
and is surely the most fair
among them."
I watched the back of Curtis Ray's head.
He didn't seem to be crying.
But Charles Darney sat shaking,
head down,
not making any noise,
just shaking.
Back at the Darneys'
women bustled in aprons
to unwrap food, set it on tables.
Thomas nudged me away from the pies.
"Come on.
We better find Curtis Ray."
He was on the back steps
reading a comic.
"Hi," said Thomas.
"I got the new Superman," said Curtis Ray,
holding it up, then noticing me.
"Hey, Eddie."

He held out the comic. "Here—
you can look."
I took the comic and we sat.
Nobody said anything.
"It was a pretty nice funeral," said Thomas, finally.
"Yeah," said Curtis Ray.
"Mom says you guys need anything,
just holler," said Thomas.
Curtis Ray bit his lip,
swallowed.
More silence.
"Superman's cool," I said.
Curtis Ray started in teasing.
"What—paperboy likes comics?"
I was glad to see him perk up.
I stood with the comic behind my back.
"I might just keep it—
I like it so much!"
Curtis lunged
but I dodged away.
"Gimme that, you little twerp!"
I took off across the yard,
him close behind.
His hip was almost good now
but he wasn't up to speed.
We circled the old pine
and were headed for the shed
when he brought me down.
I screeched,
held the comic away
as we rolled on the ground.

Curtis Ray, laughing,
finally got me pinned,
grabbed for the comic,
tore half of it from my hand.
I stopped struggling.
We looked at the pages
in his hand,
in mine,
and his face changed—
just like that
I watched it change—
from red and bright,
eyes glittering,
to crumpled and thin,
with eyes like someone
sinking
under water.

November 1938
Mom's Story

I pulled the covers up,
curled my toes around the hot-water bottle
while Mom tucked me in,
hair falling in her face
as she leaned.
Something made me think
of Curtis Ray
not getting tucked in.
"Mom, why did Annylee die?"

Mom straightened up,
frowned.
"You know.
She had cancer."
"But I mean, *why?*" I asked. "Why does anybody
gotta die?"
Mom sighed. "Everybody dies.
It's just nature.
Some die young."
She paused, watching my face.
"It ain't usual, you know."
"Tell me a story."
She smiled a little.
"Oh, you don't want a story," she said,
turning to go. "You go on to sleep."
"Please?"
Thomas, at the desk reading,
looked up for a second,
too old for stories.
Mom stopped,
leaned on the doorframe.
"Well, all right. Let me think."
"About the dead baby," I said.
Thomas turned his chair around,
gave up being cool.
Mom sat on the bed,
minding the hot-water bottle,
and in her slow, quiet way
began.
Well, it was 1922,
a real hot July.

I was eighteen.
Ma and Pa and I were in the Wilkies' parlor.
Ma had a pie.
All the neighbors were there—
wasn't hardly room to stand.
We found Ned Wilkie;
he thanked us for coming,
said Marla was fine
but couldn't leave her bed.
Sweat rolled down his face
but he didn't seem to notice
or care.
I hung back, you know,
shy.
The windows were open,
paper fans flapping.
Weren't no use—
the heat been building all day.
Forty-some hot, tired neighbors
in that parlor
and one dead baby—
enough to suffocate a person.
I stopped by the side of a window—
and I noticed the Carl boy
standing on the other side.
My heart flipped—it did—
and I looked away.
I'd heard the older girls talk
of his sly smile,
his smooth ways.
Reverend James said a few words.

Wasn't much to say.
Seemed like half the families there
had lost a babe this way,
somehow it just not wanting to stay
in this world.
Sad
but natural.
Finally folks moved on out back
to the food, the jugs of tea.
I'd just sat down when Janie Simms
touched my shoulder.
"May," she said,
"will you watch with me?"
I'd never done it before
but I nodded.
I set aside my dinner.
We slipped back through the kitchen,
and into the parlor,
darkened now.
"They put her on ice," Janie told me.
We sat for an hour,
whispering secrets,
till the Simmses stepped in.
"Janie, say good-bye now. We're going,"
I followed them to the door.
"Who will watch now?" I asked.
"I will," said a voice behind me,
low, smooth,
that Carl boy,
leaning on the wall
with a hint of that smile.

"Ned's my friend," he said.
"I told him I'd watch the night."
I found my folks.
"Can I stay?" I asked.
"Wynton Carl is watching, too."
Ma and Pa looked at each other.
"Mind, it's a sacred chore," Ma warned.
I nodded.
All night we sat in that parlor,
one dimmed lantern in the back,
the baby small, still, on the sideboard,
swaddled thin
so as not to hinder the ice.
At first we were shy, solemn,
mindful of our task.
But as the night deepened and cooled
we talked some
in whispers,
went to gaze on the baby's face,
gray and pinched in the half-light,
wondered at her passing,
pondered the fate
of that little soul.
We hauled fresh ice from the root cellar.
Wynton held the slab, freezing, waiting,
me hesitating.
This weren't no stillborn pup,
no slaughtered lamb.
Finally I slid my hands
between the ice and the babe,
lifted the tiny corpse,

surprised it was weightless,
unyielding.
Pa came at dawn. I went to find Ned.
"Marla and I are grateful, May," he said.
He walked me to the wagon,
leaned on Pa's side to talk,
but I didn't hear
because that young man Wyn
was in the doorway watching
with that hint
of a smile.
I wriggled deeper into the covers.
"And then you got married," I finished.
Mom smiled
and turned down the lamp.

November 1938
Sarah

I remember a picnic
when I was little.
Maybe three.
I was hot, lazy,
clinging, whining.
"Eddie, go play," and a little shove.
"See the sandbox?
There's Sarah."
Standing at the edge
watching Sarah busy
with water bucket, scoop,

pouring, patting, digging,
bossing,
tossing red-gold curls,
eyeing me
at the edge.
I turned away.
"Eddie Carl! You be . . .
storekeeper."
I turned back
to those laughing brown eyes,
unsure.
Sarah held out the scoop.
"Hurry up! Gimme apples—
no spots."
I took the scoop, climbed in,
and dropped to my knees,
ready to do
anything
for Sarah Mulberry.

April 1939
The News from London

In the chicken yard tossing feed,
I heard a car grind up the hill,
stop without turning in.
A man got out,
tipped his hat to the driver,
started up the drive.
It was Jozef.

I flung the rest of the feed
and trotted out to meet him.
"Jozef!" I called. "You come to shoe Hettie?"
He nodded. "If is need.
I look at her."
We walked to the barn,
to Hettie's stall.
I stroked her nose
while Jozef lifted each of her legs.
"Ah," he finally said, pointing,
"shoe is good.
This nail not here."
He set to work,
took a nail from one pocket,
a little hammer from another,
turned the nail till it laid right,
set it in the empty hole,
and started to tap.
I wanted him to talk.
"Czechoslovakia—
that's pretty near Poland, right?"
"Ya," Jozef nodded. "Is news?"
He didn't know?
"The Germans invaded!" I said.
"They say Czechoslovakia doesn't exist anymore.
Didn't you hear? On the radio?"
Jozef stopped tapping,
sat down on the barn stool.
He stared at me.
"Is true?" he asked.
"Sure! It's in the papers.

Radio said it was bound to happen
since they wouldn't give in
to Hitler.
They say—" I stopped.
"What they say?" asked Jozef. "They say
now Polska is for Mr. Hitler?"
I wished I hadn't said anything
but I nodded. "I thought
you'd already know."
Jozef went back to tapping the nail.
"I don't have radio," he said.
He patted the pocket
where he kept the piece of paper.
"I look for names.
Miss Fenton, she read when I find.
I know Nazis big trouble."
"So, you've been watching for news
of war in Poland?"
The old man shrugged.
He rested Hettie's hoof on his knee.
"To be gypsy
is to be in war.
In Czecho, in Slovakia, in Polska—
and here. Yes, here."
"But—it's not the same here," I said.
"Nobody here wants to
hurt the gypsies."
Jozef put the hammer back in his pocket,
set Hettie's leg back down.
He put a hand on my head,
thoughtful.

"No," he said,
"here, nobody hurt us."

May 1939
Pole Vault

Thomas and Gabe scraped the branch,
cleaned off the side twigs,
whittled down the knots,
worked it with their knives
till it was smooth.
"Watch this," Thomas said,
scrambling to his feet.
He stood the pole up,
taller than him by a fair bit,
placed his hands near the top,
and pulled down.
The pole wobbled,
then bowed.
"What's it for?" I asked.
"Just watch," said Gabe.
Thomas held the pole sideways
and ran.
Halfway across the yard, still running,
he planted the pole
and sailed on by it,
landing a few feet away.
"Wow!" I yelled. "Lemme try!"
But Thomas kept running,
vaulting again and again,

me tagging behind,
cheering his clumsy leaps,
begging for a turn.
Then Gabe took the pole,
running as Thomas had
but not really getting
the hang of it.
Finally Gabe held out the pole, panting.
"Okay, Squirt—
see what you can do."
I held the pole like they had
and took off across the barnyard.
I planted the pole—
and flew!
They whooped to see me soar,
and Thomas ran to pick me up
when I landed
half on my head.
"Hey, I'm going to the Olympics!" I yelled.
Thomas nodded, laughing,
swatting at the dirt in my hair.
"Danged if you ain't—
you don't kill yourself first."
Over the next days, they rigged a crossbar.
I piled straw on the landing side.
We found a ruler, marked the inches.
Gabe was a giant,
not built for pole vaulting.
He gave up after that first day.
Thomas was stocky;
never did go higher than four feet.

But I was skinny and light
and had no fear.
So they coached and hollered
as I ran, stuck the pole,
left the ground,
not listening to them
as I floated up
and over.
After three weeks, we needed a taller bar,
and Thomas borrowed a real pole
from the coach at school.
I hit five feet, then six, then seven.
Grama Lucy came one day
to dress chickens with Mom,
saw what we were doing,
threw her hands in the air.
"Mercy!
You boys are gonna kill that child!" she cried,
watching me in the air
nearly upside down.
But seeing me land in the straw,
she supposed it was all right.
I ran to her with the pole.
"Grama, you try! Come on!"
"Yeah, Gram—you can do it!" begged Thomas,
but she just laughed her big snorty laugh,
flapped her apron at us
and went back to the kitchen
shaking her head.

Yes, Ma

Grama Lucy did talk.
Whole conversations
not even needing another person.
Growing up, Dad must have figured there
weren't enough words left for him
and learned not to waste any.
When Grama came
she seemed to suck all the words
out of everybody else.
"She does rabbit on," Dad would say,
shaking his head.
I knew what he meant,
because I had plenty of opportunities
to listen.
"Wynton, did you know Effie Thompson's working
 at the Woolworth's now?"
"Yes, Ma."
"Seen her there the other day. Couldn't believe my
 eyes. Effie Thompson selling notions right there
 at the Woolworth's. Guess her widow's pension
 ain't enough. Can't imagine what trouble that
 Dulcie'll get into, all alone after school. They're
 trying Effie out at different counters, see where
 she does the best. She was selling notions that
 day, which is why I saw her. Needed some thread
 and a seam ripper. Wynton?"
"Yes, Ma."
"I don't suppose a person could repair a seam ripper.

Business end of mine got wore out and broke
off—couldn't believe my eyes. Broke right off.
Must have ripped ten thousand seams with that
thing. New one cost more than I wanted to pay,
but ain't nothing to be done about that. Got to
have a seam ripper. Wynton?"

"Yes, Ma."

"Thing is, a seam ripper's the only way to rip a
seam, 'less a body wants to spend all day picking
at threads. Agnes Strother? Never uses one.
Just uses her shears. Doing that at quilting last
month. Couldn't believe my eyes. Like using
a pitchfork to eat your eggs. Ha! That's a good
one."

"Yes, Ma."

"Could you see that, Wynton, using a pitchfork to
eat your eggs?"

"Yes, Ma."

"Wynton!"

"No, Ma. I meant . . .
no."

May 1939
In the Corn

Standing
in the new corn.
Baby green shoots
in lines long as the earth.
We'd gone to look for beans—

me, Grama Lucy, Grampa Rob.
Me a toddler,
but I knew to pull the beans,
last year's beans,
just weeds in the corn.
I liked the tractor,
the *sput-sputter* of it,
the rolling bounce,
me on Grampa's lap, helping steer,
Grama riding the hitch,
holding the back of the seat,
blue jeans turned up,
laughing on the way to find beans.
In the field, we walked the rows,
sun burning,
till Grampa with his big hankie
mopped his neck and face,
said it was enough.
At the tractor he said,
"Where's the water?"
Grama said, "I—I forgot."
One sharp slap.
Grama gasped, saw me
gaping,
stumbled to me,
scooped me up to her
smiling face
to the tears,
smiling, whispering,
"Hey now, punkin'—
it's all right."

May 1939
Sarah Mulberry

In the first grade
she was Sam,
not even all that much
a girl.
Smile as wide as her feet were long,
feet made for puddle-jumping,
fence-hopping,
running from boys.
She could bat a ball and fling a cob
with the rest of us.
In junior high, though,
she became Sarah,
still flashing that smile,
but avoiding the cob fights.
Unless she was
provoked.

July 1939
The Library

On a warm Saturday
by the window,
electric fan panning back and forth,
I read the Peoria paper,
pages riffling,
crime stories first.
Turned out Eddie the Sailor didn't

strangle those girls
and they had to let him go.
I was wondering about that,
him being named Eddie,
and what strangling
was like,
when the screen door creaked
and Jozef walked in.
Although I'd never once thought Nowy Targ
would turn up
in the *Canton Daily Ledger*
I'd kept looking.
The idea of Jozef being pals
with a camp full of beggars and thieves
had changed everything.
From the time Grama Lucy warned me
to stay clear,
I could think of nothing more fun
than being friends
with a gypsy.
So I watched for news
just in case.
He sat across from me, nodded,
gestured toward the papers.
I gave them a little shove in his direction.
We sat reading,
me glancing up every now and then.
Finally, I spoke up.
"Jozef," I whispered.
He put down his newspaper, nodded.
"Find any news

about your town in Poland?"
He shook his head.
"No," he said. "Never is news."
"I bet you miss your family," I said.
"Yes, I miss them."
I wanted to ask whether he knew any
thieves,
but it didn't seem polite.
Instead I asked, "What's it like there,
in Poland?"
He looked at me in surprise,
like he'd never heard such a question.
He took off his spectacles,
rubbed his eyebrows,
maybe trying to remember,
trying to picture it in his mind.
Finally he leaned forward.
"In Poland?
I will tell.
In Polska are mountains
filled with beauty,
such beauty,
it hurts the heart.
The brooks, they are clear.
The forests have life—
bears and big cats,
eagles,
little flowers everywhere.
I have small house in village.
I make nails
and knives,

axes,
on my stone,
sometimes pretty buttons,
always horseshoes.
In the city, Nowy Targ,
I knock on doors.
People look down on me,
but they buy.
My village is far, alone—
we have our own ways.
We make music
at feasts and weddings,
tell fortunes,
read cards or palms.
In Polska, I have wife.
I have boy.
My boy, he is man now."
He stopped, but I wanted more.
"Do you know any thieves?"
Jozef frowned.
"Always they call my people
thieves.
Is true many are clever
with stories
and quick fingers—
good skills, these. They bring
rewards"—
his face clouded—
"when they don't bring
a hanging!
Ah, you are surprised.

But for us
life is not all dancing,
music.
There are tales . . ."
I thought about this.
"So," I asked, still not understanding,
"these tales,
you think they might be
in the newspaper?"
Jozef looked down at his hands.
"Boy," he said, "you are young."
He closed the newspaper,
picked up his hat,
nodded good-bye.

September 1939
Warsaw

In the library one Saturday
the mailman brought the *Post-Dispatch*
and I was the one to unroll it.
Big headlines, photos,
all over the page
like I'd heard on the radio:
Warsaw bombed,
Germans pushing into Poland,
warplanes, air attack,
troops invading, murdering,
killing people—even killing women,
children.

I read some of the stories, then got up,
hung the paper on the rack.
Jozef's wife and son lived in the countryside,
not the city.
They were probably safe.
Probably like here.
Nothing ever happens
in the country.

October 1939
Charles Darney

Charles Darney wasn't the same
after they buried Annylee.
Not like he was crazy—
he did his work fixing tractors and corn pickers,
showed up at church,
went to town meetings.
But everyone could tell
he was pretty much just
putting one foot in front of the other
to get through the day.
That's what I heard Mom say
to Gabe's mom, Janie,
over lemon cream pie
at the Woolworth's.
"My heart aches for him," said Janie.
"They say he's always up at the graveyard."
The cemetery was over the hill from our place.
We could hear when a car turned off

to climb the road.
"That's right," said Mom.
"I see him come and go.
I sure do worry about Curtis Ray.
Seems a bit lost. But Annylee's grave
looks real nice
with flowers and what-all."
"It's been more'n a year now,"
Janie pointed out,
"and I never see Charles smile.
Just plods along
dragging that old shotgun."
She paused. "You don't think he'd ever . . ."
"I don't know," said Mom,
"but he's wore out grieving,
that's sure.
Just putting one foot in front of the other
to get through the day."

February 1940
The Church Social

The Royce twins recited
the Gettysburg Address
and had just sat down
when some kind of ruckus started
in the back of the church.
I twisted my neck along with everybody else
to get a look.
Old Merle Stanton

was trying to keep a young lady
from coming up the aisle.
He had ahold of her sleeve.
I whispered, "Grama, who *is* that?"
Grama Lucy angled her head down,
looking through the top part of her glasses,
but even with her best
double-barreled stare
she couldn't make out who it was.
On the other side of me
Grampa Rob shook his head.
"Ain't nobody from here," he said.
The girl started in squealing.
"Sir, I will thank you to let me pass!
I understand this is a public recital
and I am entitled to participate!"
She and Merle had arm-wrestled
halfway up the aisle by then
and it was clear she was strong—
stronger than old Merle, at least.
Seeing it was no use, Merle let go of her sleeve
but not without a last word.
"Miss," he huffed, "you are
not on the program,
but we don't aim to leave nobody out."
To folks' amazement, the young miss
stopped in her tracks,
smiled a big lipsticked smile,
laid a white-gloved hand
on Merle's arm.
"Well, now," she cooed,

"aren't you a sweet ol' bear!"
Then she flounced on up to the front.
Dulcie Thompson was standing there
waiting to sing
but hied on back to her seat
when she saw what was coming.
The young woman turned
to face the congregation.
The church fell silent
at the sight of her,
tall and willowlike
in a flowery skirt and blouse
with a little jacket to match.
She had bright-painted cheeks,
dark curls out to here,
and a little straw hat
with paper flowers
and a bumblebee on the brim.
She raised both hands,
making little hello motions.
"Howdy, all!
My name is Leonora DuPrette.
I am just thrilled to bring you
my vocal performance this evening,
which I shall accompany
with gestures
which I have learned through study
at a highly respected studio of the arts
in New York City."
While we all gaped like caught fish
she started in

singing a little posy-pansy song,
mincing around in her high-heeled shoes,
swaying this way and that,
yodeling away
and looking so silly
we couldn't help but enjoy it.
Grama Lucy shook her head,
trying not to smile,
but smiled a little anyways.
Grampa Rob frowned.
Then the girl was swinging her hips
and the song that had seemed sweet
a minute before
took on a low, growly sound.
The congregation started in
buzzing.
Oh, boy, I thought, as Leonora DuPrette
unbuttoned her jacket
and in the midst of all that hip motion
commenced to swing it up
and around her head.
Grama Lucy leaned into my ear,
fanning herself with a hankie.
"Jiminy Cricket!" she whispered,
"what on earth . . ."
Other heads were wagging,
and as that little flowered jacket
went sailing over the head of the organist,
one whole row across the aisle stood up,
gathered their wraps to leave.
Grampa Rob leaned across me,

said, "Lucy—
we've seen enough."
But Grama paid no attention—
she was staring,
open-mouthed.
The girl turned her back,
bent over,
pulled off her hat.
When she straightened up and turned around,
we saw she'd pulled her hair off, too!
She flashed a big red smile,
waving her hat in one hand,
her hair in the other.
Grama gasped.
Everybody gasped.
Then someone yelled, "It's Leo!
It's Leo Strother!"
I looked closely—
at the painted mouth,
the nose and eyes,
the slicked-back blond hair,
shoulders that were a little too broad after all
for a lady,
and the white-gloved hands
that suddenly seemed
enormous.
It *was* Leo!
Grampa stood. "Lucy! Eddie!
Get your coats."
But then the crowd roared.
Women shrieked and cackled,

rushing to pinch Leo's cheek.
Men chortled,
pounded him on the back.
Every last one of us had been
fooled.
Merle Stanton looked on, beaming;
he'd been in on it all along.
I looked at Grampa Rob
scowling.
But Grama was staring at Leo,
her mouth open in surprise,
her breath caught up like
she couldn't believe her eyes.
Then she let out a great guffaw
and laughed till she had to put her hankie
to her eyes.
"Well! I never," she hooted.
"I never!"
She turned to Grampa Rob,
still wiping away tears.
"You go on home!
Effie will give us a ride."
Grampa snatched up his coat,
strode away,
and Grama said to me,
"Come on, Eddie.
Let's go tell that Leo
what a bad, bad boy he is!"

February 1940
The Note

Waiting for the bell,
we leaned on the fifth-graders' fence.
Stump Keal had a baseball card,
Hank Greenberg.
"Yeah?" said Little Buss Burton,
"I got a Jimmie Foxx."
Stinky said, "I got them
and three Lou Gehrigs!"
but nobody believed him.
A few yards away
the girls were jumping rope.
Two turned,
the others waited to jump.
Sarah Mulberry stood in line
chanting with the others:
Teddy Bear, Teddy Bear, turn out the light.
Shirlynn Gump skipped out
and Sarah skipped in,
pigtails flying.
Little Buss shoved at my shoulder.
"Haw! Eddie Carl's in love."
Little Buss wasn't little—
he was the son of
Big Buss Burton—
and the way he was growing,
he'd be a Big Buss, too.
He was loud
so I walked away,

him following, whispering,
"I'm gonna tell her.
I'm gonna tell her you love her."
I told him to shut up
but he kept bugging me.
"Okay then, Carl—
I dare you to tell her she's a
homely sow."
All that day Buss rode me.
In arithmetic he made a show
of writing a note,
not easy for him,
pushing his stubby pencil
nearly through the paper
and erasing
more than writing.
When he finished,
he turned it so I could see.
Sarah Molberry is a homily sow.
Sined
Eddie Carl.
He folded it in a tiny square,
wrote "Sarah" on the front,
and when Mr. Atwood turned away
he tapped the kid in front of him.
I thought about grabbing it
but Mr. Atwood had a rule:
anyone caught with a note
had to read it out loud.
The next kid was Stinky.
He read "Sarah" on the front,

turned back, saw the panic on my face,
and stuck the note in his pocket.
Good ol' Stinky!
He wasn't so dumb.
For the rest of the hour
we played Around the World,
a mathematics game.
If you answered right
you moved up a desk.
Long as you answered right,
you got more questions
and got to keep moving.
When I moved past Buss
he made an ugly face.
"Yer friend's gonna get it,"
he whispered.
At the end of class
we gathered our books,
stood to leave.
"Just a minute!" barked Mr. Atwood.
"Sylvester Dean has something to read us."
Stinky glanced at me,
looked a bit pale.
"I—I don't—" he stammered, "I mean—"
"You know the rule.
Turn your pockets out."
Miserably, Stinky put his hands in both pockets,
pulled them out,
and a miracle happened.
Nothing was there,
just a couple of big holes.

We tried not to look like
we couldn't believe our eyes.
Little Buss thought fast.
I saw him scan the floor.
"Hey!" he said, pointing.
He pounced on the dirty square,
handed it to Mr. Atwood,
who opened it, read it,
looked at me.
The class waited;
my face burned.
"Eddie Carl," he demanded,
"spell *homely.*"
"H-o-m-e-l-y," I obliged.
He frowned.
"All right, class. Run along."
As we filed out
he wadded up the note,
tossed it in the waste can.
But when Little Buss reached the door
Mr. Atwood called after him.
"Mr. Burton, I'll see you after school.
You can wash the floors."

June 1940
Churchill

"Shush!" I warned
as Thomas banged the screen door.
"It's the prime minister

of England!
I already missed most of it."
Thomas shrugged,
tramping on into the kitchen,
where I could hear him opening cupboards.
I twisted the radio dial
to get rid of the crackling.
Winston Churchill sounded weary to the bone,
but calm,
fatherly.
His accent made him hard to understand.
In England they were probably
used to it.
He said he was determined to fight.
I hoped he meant it.
If Hitler conquered Europe
we'd be next.
"If we fail," he went on,
"then the whole world . . .
will sink
into the abyss
of a new Dark Age."

July 1940
Live and Let Live

People argued whether
America should go to war.
Live and let live, some said.
If other countries want to squabble,

why should we fight
and die?
Seemed like everyone I knew
felt the same way.
One day Mom was making biscuits
and I asked her,
"Why shouldn't we fight?
We help our neighbors—
it's the same, right?"
Mom sighed,
sprinkled more flour,
rolled the dough just a little—
not like pie.
She turned a jam jar upside down
to cut circles.
"It's not that simple," she finally said,
dropping the rounds in a pan.
"You probably wouldn't die
for your neighbor,
would you?"
She put the pan in the oven,
started wiping the flour off the table.
"If Dawsons' was on fire
you'd try to help,
but you wouldn't walk into the fire,
would you?"
That didn't seem right.
"No, 'cause I'm not brave enough,"
I said.
"I still think I ought."
Mom gave a couple of yanks on the pump

to fill the mixing bowl with water
and put it in the sink to soak.
"Well, yes," she admitted,
"it might be right
but it would be pointless.
What good is it to anyone
if you die, too?"
I wasn't ready to give up.
"But if I did try to save them
and we all got out,
everyone would say I done right.
I'd be a hero!"
Mom dried her hands on her apron
and put them on my shoulders.
"But sweetie, you have to understand,"
she said, kissing the top of my head,
"in a war, it's not just one person
taking the risk.
And the people who decide
aren't risking their own lives.
Thousands of young men
might die."
I squirmed away.
"But I read that Hitler's trying
to get rid of Jewish people
and gypsies.
I read they're
arresting them."
She let me go.
"Well, those are rumors."
She took a wet dishcloth,

gave the table a few swipes.
"And I sincerely doubt
those rumors are true."
She draped the cloth over the pump handle,
wiped her red hands on her apron.
"Eddie, it would be foolish
for us to join the war
till we know there's a real threat.
Go on now—
tell your dad and Thomas to wash up."
I wanted to argue
but kept it to myself.
Didn't Mom listen to the news?
There was a threat, all right.
The abyss of a new Dark Age.
If that wasn't a threat,
I didn't know what was.

August 1940
The Tin

I remember baking cookies,
Grama Lucy showing Thomas
to roll just so,
him frowning, pressing too hard.
"Try again, honey."
I played at their feet,
too little to help,
flour on hands, face, floor,
laughing, slipping,

running and sliding
on my knees, singing,
"Roll-l-l-l me,
roll-l-l me on over!"
into the pantry, into the shelves, where
bottles clanked and tins tottered.
"Eddie, be careful!"
"I will!"
I set things aright
—and there, on the lowest shelf in the back,
a tin I didn't know.
I pulled off the lid, humming,
roll me over to Pottinger's farm . . .
Opened: money—
bills in a fat roll.
I put it back,
all the way back,
where nobody knew,
feeling like a thief,
not knowing why.
On my feet, I ran to the table,
face hot, singing, shouting,
"Roll me on over to Pottinger's farm!
Roll me to Pottinger's farm!"

August 1941
The Squirrel Hunt

It was a little damp for hunting
but Curtis Ray said squirrels

let down their guard
after a rain.
So after chores and breakfast
we got our .22s and some shells,
Thomas and me,
and started down the hill
toward the bridge,
a bit of a sun coming up
through the clouds.
At the bridge
Curtis Ray and Gabe were waiting.
Curt dropped his cigarette,
ground the butt with his heel.
"Oughtn't set a bad example,"
he said as we walked up.
"Too late," I shot back. "You know,
more doctors smoke Camels
than any other cigarette."
The others laughed.
Curt said, "Yeah, but Old Golds
give you a pick-me-up.
And if you don't get a thrill—"
I chimed in with him: "We'll pay the bill—
and double!"
"Shut up," said Thomas,
"you'll scare the squirrels."
We shut up.
I didn't much care
if we ate squirrel tonight,
but I knew Curt did.
He and Charles Darney

pretty much lived out of a
frying pan
since Annylee died.
We walked along the road,
then cut into the woods
toward the rusted old school bus
abandoned there.
The path was muddy,
the brush wet,
so we walked single file,
trying to keep dry.
Two hours later we doubled back
to hunker in the bus,
rain pounding the roof,
windows mostly shut, door open,
so aside from Curt's Old Golds,
it wasn't too bad in there.
Gabe had two squirrels,
Thomas one.
I hadn't even taken a shot.
Curt had shot wild all morning.
Talking, we gave the World Series
to Joltin' Joe and the Yankees
and decided
if you had to die
guillotine was best;
after that, electric chair,
and both better than
hanging.
Now we were on the war.
Gabe was excited.

"If Americans had been there
to sink the *Bismarck*," he said,
"it wouldn't a took so long."
Thomas agreed. "We'd a done it
with fighter planes
and bombers,
from the sky—
forget the battleships."
Curtis objected. "What? Battleships are best!
Takes one to sink one."
"But it was a fighter plane
torpedoed the rudder," I put in,
"slowed her down.
After that the *Bismarck*
was a sitting duck."
"Yeah," said Thomas, "in planes
you're in and out, fast.
And you can send 'em in waves.
Boats are slow."
Curtis Ray wasn't convinced.
"Yeah, but how'd the planes get there?
On aircraft carriers.
And it's better to be on a boat.
Then if the Germans hit,
you can swim."
"Well," said Gabe, "we get in the war,
you'll get your chance.
Bet it won't be long now."
Curt nodded. "Dad says things'll get tough here,
we go to war."
"Not as tough as over there," I said.

"Jozef says in Poland
the Nazis can get you out of bed
middle of the night
and shoot you, no reason."
Curtis Ray turned and spat out the door.
"Ya know, Shorty,
'no reason' might mean something
a little different
to Mirga."
"What're you talking about?" I asked. "What *reason*
would they have
to put even little kids
in concentration camps?"
He blew a smoke ring
and considered.
"Well," he said, "first of all,
I wouldn't take the word of no gypsy
in the middle of Illinois
about what's going on in Poland.
And second of all,
you gotta admit
how Hitler and them
got their hands full
with all them Jews and gypsies.
I'm not saying anyone should get shot
for no reason, but
puttin' them all in one place
makes a certain kind of sense.
Think about it.
That's why they're called
concentration camps:

they concentrate them
in one place
so they'll be out of the way
during the war."
Gabe and Thomas looked at me.
"You're crazy," I said, "or you're a Nazi.
You ask me,
unless we want Hitler
over here deciding
who's good enough to live,
we need to get in there."
"Ha!" Curtis laughed,
threw down his cigarette,
tapped it with his toe.
"I'll tell you this, Paperboy:
If I'm a Nazi,
then I guess we got us a fair number
of Nazis
right here in Ellisville."

August 1941
Spoon River

A tradition he called it—
Grampa Rob—
walking the Spoon
the year you turn twelve.
His farm was on the river
near a bend,
where a couple times a year

a man can walk across
under water
if things are just right.
You find a big rock,
big as you can carry,
and wade in.
In the middle you'll go under,
but if you keep on,
hold your breath,
you'll make it to the other side—
most times.
I'd watched Thomas do it.
Now I was twelve,
and I didn't want to go.
Dad told Grampa
leave it be.
But Grampa kept ragging,
"Time to be a man,"
and one day at his place, he said,
"Let's go, boy."
Grampa went first.
He barely went under, tall as he was.
He went slow,
weighted down and blind
in the river water,
foot-feeling around rocks and slime.
I counted the seconds.
Finally the gray-bald head
broke the surface
and a minute later
he staggered up the other side,

dripping,
still lugging that rock.
"Hoo! Ain't nothin' to it!
Come on, boy!"
It took time finding a rock.
I couldn't settle on one
till Grampa hollered.
I felt small
shuffling into the Spoon
with my rock.
When my nose hit the water
I stopped,
shivering.
Grampa shouted "You a girl?"
I heaved a breath
and went under
but shot up again, arms thrashing,
gulping air.
Six times, six rocks,
Grampa pacing, railing,
me shivering,
water on my face
might have been tears.
Grampa drove me home, silent.
To Mom and Dad he said,
"Here's your little man."

Halloween

In the barn at Royces' orchard party
lightbulbs blazed
from the rafters,
squaredancers twirled
to the fiddles and jugs,
children ran, sticky
with taffy apples,
adults sipped coffee and cider.
Stinky and I raced around
bobbing for apples,
swinging from ropes
into the hay,
making scarecrow heads
from paper bags.
I grabbed popcorn balls from a bowl,
tossed one to Stinky.
"Let's go outside," I said,
"see what Thomas is doing."
Lately Thomas had been
ditching me
when other friends were around.
We wandered into the orchard,
the music fading.
This Halloween was fine and dry,
moon nearly full.
Chilly, the night smelled just right,
dry leaves, cut hay,
bonfire.

Sounded right, too,
wind rustling,
owls calling.
We heard laughter
from back in the trees.
"Let's spy," Stinky whispered.
We crept closer
till we could see
Thomas and Curtis Ray
and Pauline LeBeau.
Thomas was talking,
excited.
"Everybody's jumping in now.
Maybe even this Mussolini guy."
"Yeah," said Curtis Ray,
"he joins up with Hitler,
they'll stomp England and France."
Pauline tossed her ponytail. "Well,
long as we stay out of it."
"Right," said Curtis Ray. "Them
Nazis'd knock the shit
out of us."
"Curtis Ray! Mind your mouth."
Pauline giggled,
gave him a little poke
in the chest.
Curtis Ray put a cigarette
between his lips.
"Okay—like this?" he said,
lighting up.
Pauline looked impressed.

Thomas couldn't beat that.
I nudged Stinky. "Curt's dad doesn't know
he smokes.
Wonder what he'd do if he saw."
Stinky knew.
"Whip his butt, that's what."
Thomas tried again.
"We go in,
I'm signing up," he declared.
Pauline turned to him.
"No—and get yourself killed?"
Thomas stood straighter. "I wouldn't.
I'd be a flier—
a fighter pilot."
Curtis Ray made an effort
with a quick "Me, too!"
but Pauline was gazing
at Thomas.
"Then I'll go, too!"
she said. "I'll be a nurse."
Thomas smiled at her.
"That'd be swell."
"Hey, let's go dance,"
put in Curtis Ray.
Pauline grabbed Thomas by the arm
and pulled. "Okay, let's go!"
She and Thomas ran for the barn,
leaving Curt
to stamp out his cigarette
and run after them.
Stinky elbowed me and giggled.

"Thomas got a girl!"
I nodded,
but that wasn't where
my mind was.
If there was a war,
Thomas might go.

November 1941
Dr. Jekyll and Mr. Hyde

I was moving slow.
I'd been home with a cold,
still coughing junk from my chest.
Dad and I were in town.
We finished at the hardware store
and walked past the
movie house,
stopping in front of the poster,
me with my mouth open
partly from awe,
partly because I couldn't breathe
through my nose.
I knew he was just an actor,
Spencer Tracy,
but it gave me the shivers:
Dr. Jekyll and Mr. Hyde.
"Want to go in?" said Dad.
"Sure!" I breathed.
There was always a line Saturdays.
I saw Sarah Mulberry

and her friend Shirlyn Gump
join the line.
They saw me
and put their heads together,
giggling.
We shuffled toward the ticket booth.
Some little kids ahead of us,
a boy and a girl,
raggedy in thin coats, excited,
hopped up and down
against the cold.
"Gypsies," said Dad.
Near the booth the girl turned,
searched her pockets,
walked back along the line
staring at the sidewalk.
The boy reached the window
where Clara Stubee
glared down.
"How many?" Clara barked.
"Uh, two—but my sister
dropped her money," he stammered.
"Step aside!" Clara ordered.
The boy stood to the side
while the girl kept looking.
When it was our turn
Dad thrust two quarters under the glass.
The girl came to her brother,
in tears.
I looked up at Dad.
"Lost her money," I said.

"Best not get involved," he said.

He grabbed our tickets
and we walked away,
but as we went in I turned back to see
Sarah Mulberry
dig in her purse,
and hand the girl
a quarter.

December 1941
A Date Which Will Live in Infamy

At 11:25, the whole of Hessing Elementary
crowded into the first-grade room.
I clumped with the other eighth graders
at the back wall.
Miss Dell stood in front,
fiddled with the radio knobs.
The squawks and hisses finally gave way
to the voice of President Roosevelt.
The speech was short.
"Yesterday," he said, "December 7, 1941,
a date which will live in infamy,
the United States of America
was suddenly and deliberately
attacked
by naval and air forces of the
Empire of Japan. . . .
I ask that Congress declare that
since the unprovoked and dastardly attack . . .

a state of war has existed
between the United States
and the Japanese Empire."
There was more,
but we older kids
didn't listen.
Excited, we shoved and
whispered.
The teachers
told us to hush.
A couple girls cried.
Stinky nudged his way over to me,
his eyes wide.
"War!" he said,
and I nodded.
The Japanese had bombed
Pearl Harbor.

May 1942
Cob War

Thomas inched on his belly
toward the edge of the hayloft,
Stinky and I close behind.
Grampa's loft was perfect
for swinging and jumping:
two different levels
with ledges and sills
and extra ropes he put up
just for us and our pals.

He said ropes were for real boys,
ladders for sissies.
"Here they come," Thomas whispered.
"Get the bombs!"
I shoved the gunnysack forward
and we all grabbed a couple.
No ordinary corncobs, these—
they were state-of-the-art,
handcrafted,
lovingly watered
for weight and sting,
dipped in manure,
clean at one end for a good grip,
foul on the other
for the ultimate impact.
Cob bombs.
Below, Gabe and Curtis Ray
shouldered the barn door open,
peered in,
heavily armed,
a cob in one hand,
the other holding
a shirttail full of extras.
Stinky and I started up,
but Thomas grabbed us,
whispered, "Wait!"
We froze.
The intruders heard nothing
and relaxed.
"We beat 'em to it!
Let's get up there," said Gabe.

They headed toward the ladder.
Thomas yelled, "Now!"
We jumped to our feet and let fly.
Thomas's bombs
zipped past from behind.
"Bombs away!" Stinky screeched,
always glad to make noise.
We hurled with both hands,
grabbing cobs
fast as we could.
Down below they dove behind bales of hay,
yelling and grunting
as the manure splattered.
We saw our chance—
Thomas, supercharged,
tossed the sack down first,
then slid down a rope
with a Tarzan yell.
I belly flipped over the edge,
landed on my feet,
while Stinky bumbled down the ladder,
sprawled at the bottom,
and took a few cobs
in the back.
Too late,
we saw our mistake—
we were sitting ducks.
Cobs rained from both sides.
Safe behind bales,
Gabe and Curt cackled with glee
as they hurled one cob after another.

Curtis Ray taunted us:
"So much for the big bombs!"
Thomas took a cob on the ear,
yelled in pain.
We grabbed the sack,
ran for the door,
the others at our heels.
"Every man for himself!"
We scattered,
guerrillas and snipers,
sneaking behind the outhouse,
chasing down the driveway,
lying in wait beside the shed,
pausing in the open
only to scoop up
ammunition.
I was in the side yard
hotfooting it for the porch,
Gabe closing in on me,
when dead ahead
Grama swung around the corner of the house
with a basket of laundry.
A filthy cob flew past me,
splatted into the basket.
I stopped so fast
Gabe barreled straight into me
and we both sprawled
at Grama's feet.
She was so mad she sputtered.
"Blast you rascals!" she yelled.
Pretty strong language,

for her.
"What did I tell you
about flinging those cobs!
That Johnston boy
in the hospital—
a blinded eye and two teeth out!
Didn't Harvey Ketters get his windows broke?
Them cobs are not toys!
They're dangerous!"
She grabbed us both by an ear,
yanked us up.
"Git on up to the house!
I should take the yardstick to you.
You can just do this laundry over.
Go on, now—
git!
You, too, Gabe."
While we slunk on up to the house
Grama marched off across the farmyard,
fuming, looking for the others.
But they'd hightailed it
when they heard the yelling.
So Gabe and I were POWs,
former enemies,
captured and forced
to scrub and wring and hang
our captor's clothes.
Gabe didn't seem to mind.
"Gabe, why aren't you mad?
This stinks! It ain't fair."
Gabe's big fingers

spread some dripping overalls
between the rollers of the wringer
and began to turn the crank.
"I'll tell you why," he said,
"but it's a secret.
You can't tell no one, okay?"
I nodded.
"I've decided to join up," he said,
"and when you think about
the war,
this here just seems kind of funny,
your grandma telling us
how dangerous it is
to throw cobs."
I was stunned.
"Join up! But why?
You don't have to go.
Farmers don't have to."
The flattened overalls came out the other side,
dropped into an empty washtub,
and Gabe started another pair through.
"Well, I been thinking a lot
about what's going on
with Hitler and the Nazis
and all.
And in the Pacific—looks bad.
President keeps asking
every able-bodied man
to enlist.
Heck, Eddie—
you said so yourself

more than once,
talking about Jozef's
family over in Poland."
"Well, I—I know.
But you shouldn't listen to me—
I'm just a kid!
I wasn't thinking about *you* going over.
Listen to your folks.
They know better."
Gabe shook his head.
"I'm eighteen, Eddie.
I should be making my own mind up.
And I've pretty well made it up.
Soon as graduation's over
I'm signing up."

June 1942
The Decision

"Your mom's gonna kill you, Gabe," I said,
hustling along Main Street
behind him, Thomas, and Curtis Ray.
The post office came into view
and we stopped at the windows,
the posters.
Uncle Sam, jacket flung down, fists ready,
eagle on his shoulder:
Defend Your Country—Enlist Now in the United
States Army.
A bare-chested sailor, biceps bulging,

hefting a torpedo:
Man the Guns—Join the Navy.
A screaming eagle, diving with fighter planes:
Wings over America—Air Corps U.S. Army.
Thomas turned to his friends.
"You guys sure?"
Gabe and Curtis Ray nodded.
Thomas shook his head,
began to pace.
"Damn, I wish I could go—
but you know I can't.
I got this chance for college.
My folks'd kill me—"
Gabe stopped him.
"Tom, we know," he said.
"Curt and me ain't going
to college.
The farm'll be here,
when I get back.
And you know
my folks don't really need me."
Gabe had three brothers.
They'd been over it
a million times.
Gabe wanted college, too,
to study agriculture,
take over the farm someday.
But there was no money for that.
Curtis Ray had no plans
for college.
After Annylee died,

I don't think he and Charles Darney
thought much about
his future.
Besides,
it was his duty to enlist.
I looked at Curtis Ray staring
at the poster,
the snazzy uniform.
I knew he couldn't wait to turn up
in town
looking like that.
Thomas stopped pacing.
He looked at me.
"You know, Eddie,
Gabe's got a point.
College would still be there, too,
when I got back."
"And," he went on,
"you all have to get along
without me either way,
I go to college or join up."
He waited—for what?
For me to say he was right?
"Thomas—that's crazy!
You can't!"
"Yes, I can," he said,
"I have to."
Gabe tried to frown
but seemed to be fighting
a grin.
"Tom," he said, "you should wait—

talk to your folks."
Thomas shot back, "You talking to yours?"
determination, excitement
in his voice.
Thomas and Gabe looked
at each other,
their grins growing large.
"Okay, then!" Curt stepped between them,
clapped a hand
on both their shoulders.
"We're all going in!
We'll be together—
one for all and all for one!"
The three of them stood there,
eyes glinting
on the brink of their dare.
Thomas turned to me.
"Wish me luck, Buddy."
I shook his hand, stomach churning.
Don't do it. Don't go.
The thought of him going—
my heart hammered,
but somewhere in me
a thrill
deep as I'd ever known.
I wanted him to go.
Even more,
I wanted to go, too.
I stood on the sidewalk watching
as they opened the door
and disappeared.

June 1942
The Physical

A week later
I was hoeing potatoes
when Thomas came around the
side of the house,
a slump in his walk.
I leaned on my hoe.
"How'd it go?"
He and the others had gone
for their physicals.
Thomas shook his head.
"They wouldn't take Curtis Ray."
The three of them and one other boy
had stood in line.
Doc Gordon weighed and measured,
checked ears, noses, eyes,
opened mouths,
marked his charts.
Hearts were fine;
blood pressures fine.
Things were winding up
when the doc said, "Okay, then
let's see y'all
touch your toes."
The boys had bobbed down,
reached their toes briefly—
except for Curtis Ray,
who couldn't make it
more than halfway.

The doc looked surprised,
then sorry.
"I forgot about your hip, boy."
Curt couldn't believe it.
"But Doc—
that was a long time ago.
I can do it, I'm sure!
I just gotta get
warmed up."
He bent his legs,
tried again, grunting,
but he couldn't do it.
Doc wouldn't budge.
Said a lack of flexibility
put a soldier in danger,
his fellow soldiers, too.
He had no choice:
Curtis Ray was classified as 4F,
physically unfit
to serve in the armed forces.
I couldn't believe it.
"But he can do chin-ups, push-ups,
run a mile—
he don't even limp!"
Thomas shrugged.
"Doc knows all that."
"How's he taking it?" I asked.
"Pretty broke up," Thomas said.
"He was fixed on
sticking with Gabe.
And he's afraid what folks'll say

when he don't go."
"Lots of guys aren't going," I said.
"Yeah, but they're going to college,
working the farms.
Curt says he feels like a
good-for-nothing."
I shook my head.
"Well, he tried," I said. "What more
could he do?"

September 1942
The Bus

Pat drove the winding dirt roads
like he had for forty years,
kids yelling, bouncing,
hanging on around the curves,
Stinky and me in the back
like always,
him rattling on,
this time about making money.
"See, I could get people to give me
their old tools,
stuff they don't use anymore.
Then I shine 'em up and sell 'em!
That antiques place out toward Avon?
They sell stuff like this!
People from Chicago buy it."
Sarah Mulberry
was in the seat ahead,

talking
the way she does,
everything in motion.
I was a foot and a half from the
back of her neck,
her ponytail
whipping left and right
as she talked,
some long reddish wisps
hanging here and there.
On that day the bus skidded sideways,
landed nose forward in a ditch,
all of us jolted, surprised—
probably the first time silence happened
on Pat's bus.
"Ever'one okay?" he asked.
Aside from Bucky Barnes's split lip
and a bump on Maisie Edson's forehead,
everyone was fine.
"This here's an emergency," said Stinky,
hopeful,
nodding toward the back door.
Emergency?
Evacuate!
I thought about Thomas
away at the air base—
probably learning emergency drills,
women and children first.
"Stinky, open the door! Girls first!
Off the bus!"
Stinky leaped for the door,

swung it wide.
I stood at attention by Sarah's row:
"Go on! I'll wait
till everyone's off."
Sarah stopped in the doorway. "But—"
"Quick!" I said. "The fuel could explode!"
And with a shove
I saved Sarah Mulberry's life,
sending her out the door
into half a foot
of dirty ditch water.
Pat heard the screech,
elbowed his way to the back.
"What the—"
Sarah sat in the ditch,
gasping, muddy,
face plastered with wet strands
of hair.
She stood up yelling.
"You stupid creep!
You did that on purpose!"
I felt the burn rise
from my gut to my flattop
seeing her there
all ruin,
climbing up the slippery side of the ditch.
Next she would cry.
But Sarah didn't cry—
she laughed.
Standing there dripping,
she wiped the hair off her face

and laughed
like a man.
"I hate you, Eddie Carl!" she hollered
with her big wide grin.
"I hate you!
And I'm gonna get you for this!"

September 1942
Dear Thomas

Dear Thomas,
How is it there in Nashville?
Congratulations for getting classed
as pilot.
Do they let you fly anything yet?
You won't believe this,
but I've just been flying!
Today at Cuba junction
the crop duster was giving rides in his plane
and Grama asked if I wanted to fly.
His rates were $9.00 an hour.
Grama said, "Take us up for ten minutes."
We went straight west
till we hit on a line with our place.
We circled the spoil banks
and then our time was up.
You should have seen the grin
on Grama's face.
We flew about 11½ minutes all told,
250 feet up by the altimeter,

at 65 miles per hour.
I figured up it was pretty dear
riding with rates like these.
10 min = $1.50
1 hour = $9.00
24 hours = $216.00
1 week = $1,512.00
Gabe is in New Jersey.
Janie says he's eager to get to Europe.
Go get 'em, Ace.
Your brother,
Edward Kenneth Carl

October 1942
Town Meeting

I was sitting with the Banter High ninth grade
in the back corner
of the town hall meeting room
getting a lesson in civics
when Charles Darney came in
late,
shuffled up to the front,
stood twisting his hat,
cleared his throat,
seemed to remember just in time
not to spit.
He shifted foot to foot,
finally spoke up.
"They's gophers in the graveyard."

He looked satisfied and sat down.
Merle Stanton banged the gavel.
"We're still doing old business, Charles," he said,
"and them gophers is new business."
"Ain't nothin' new about 'em,"
Effie Thompson pointed out.
Merle banged again. "Effie, you're out of order."
Giggles from our corner.
"Any more old business?" Merle asked,
giving plenty of time.
When there wasn't any,
he looked annoyed.
"Then we'll move on to new business.
Any new business?"
Charles Darney hauled himself to his feet again.
"They's gophers in the graveyard."

April 1943
The Question

Dad and I cut stalks in the south seven
and had just quit for the day.
Filthy, tired,
we walked home along the fences,
not saying much.
Where the county road cuts through—
the road to Grama and Grampa's—
I asked,
"How come you got your own farm?
You could have stayed,

farmed with Grampa."
We trudged across half a field
before Dad spoke.
"We got our differences," he said,
and that was all he had to say.

July 1943
Dear Thomas

Dear Thomas,
Come Tuesday, it's a year
you're gone.
Pretty soon, you'll have your wings.
Mom and Dad are telling everyone.
They're really proud
but please don't even bump your elbow on the
cockpit
or Mom will feel it in her bones
and we'll have to pray extra.
Now that you're back in Illinois,
Gabe's in Tennessee.
He's in the Army Rangers.
Janie says he's the best shot
in his platoon.
I got third in the last pest killing contest.
I had one rat tail, two sparrows,
and a mouse.
Little Buss got first with six spatzies,
but I found out he paid Stump
to give him four.

I'm reading *Dave Dawson at Singapore*.
I'm most the way done.
Thanks for sending it.
I can't wait to see you next week!
I'm excited about coming to the base.
Your brother,
Eddie Carl
p.s. When I get there,
any chance we could go for a spin?
Sneak one of those babies out
after dark?
Do they keep the bombs loaded?
We could fly over school,
drop a few.

July 1943
Chanute Field

I hopped off the bus,
glad to stretch after six hours
and two buses.
I saw Thomas
before he saw me.
It surprised me
how grown-up he looked
in uniform.
He was staring at the ground,
looking glum.
For a second I was afraid
he didn't want me there.

When he saw me, though,
he grinned big.
"You made it!" he said,
pounding my back. "Hungry?"
I nodded.
"We can get something in the mess."
He pointed across the base
to a long, low building.
On the way, some of the guys who passed us
saluted Thomas
and he saluted back.
He had his silver wings now,
second lieutenant.
I knew it didn't have anything to do with me
but I couldn't help being proud
he was my brother.
I matched my stride to his.
Thomas saw it.
"You're getting tall, Buddy," he said,
"and look at those feet!"
That made me laugh. "Heck," I said,
"with the ration on,
Mom buys my shoes big
so they last."
I wanted to see everything on the base.
"Where do they keep the fighters?" I asked,
looking around.
The dark look returned to Thomas's face.
He pulled a paper out of his pocket.
"We got our assignments yesterday . . ."
He held out the paper.

Scanning it, I saw that he was going
to New Mexico to train—
on a B-24 bomber.
"But that's great!" I said. "I mean,
it wasn't sure you'd even get pilot—
right?"
Thomas nodded. "I know—
I'm glad I got pilot—
but geez, Eddie.
Flying those bombers
is like flying a hay wagon.
You can't do nothing with them.
I wanted my own plane.
In a bomber
there's a whole crew.
I'd be responsible."
We reached the mess hall,
filled with clamor and clatter,
a couple hundred guys eating
at long tables.
Thomas steered me toward the line.
"Why do you think you got bomber?" I asked.
Thomas handed me a tray.
"Well, they never give you a reason.
I heard smaller guys
get the fighters
'cause the cockpits are cramped.
But my pal Dickenson's a shrimp
and he's going to New Mexico, too."
I wanted Thomas to be happy.
I knew he dreamed

of cutting up in a fighter,
being an ace—and what the heck—
winning the war
all by himself.
I thought about him in a bomber.
"You know, they probably want good leaders
in the bombers," I pointed out,
"and even if you don't want it,
you'll be a good captain."
"I don't know," Thomas said,
"but I'll try."
"Besides," I went on, "with a crew,
you won't be alone
if something happens."
I laughed. "And you'll be safer—
no loop-the-loops!"
Thomas sighed.
"Right."
The rest of that day,
Thomas showed me all over the base.
He showed me a B-24
and I sat in the pilot's seat.
I saw the fire ax,
the bomb bay.
I couldn't believe how big the thing was
from outside,
and then how small the spaces were
for all the gunners.
You'd have to have guts
to ride in the gunner's basket
hanging off the front.

We watched planes take off and land
and after dinner we went to the movies,
right there on the base.
The next morning after breakfast and chapel,
it was time for me to get back on the bus.
I hated to leave.
The bus lurched up, opened its doors.
"Well, 'bye, Squirt," Thomas said.
"See you at home in a few weeks. And hey—
keep an eye on the sky.
Soon as I get the go-ahead,
I'll fly over,
show you my stuff."
Thomas handed me my bag
but didn't let go.
"You know, Eddie," he said,
"you got me thinking—
about the bomber,
about not being alone.
I'm gonna remember that."
He gave me a smack on the back.
"Thanks, Bud.
I mean it."

July 1943
  Flyover

Early morning,
soft rain dampened the dust
as I followed Dad to the barn.

Cows don't care about rain;
they want milking anyways.
We hunkered down on stools
leaning into the smell of hide.
Morning milking's quiet,
slow.
Lucky, or we might not have heard
the drone,
no more than a skeeter buzz,
then deeper and louder,
till we looked up,
startled,
and raced out of the barn.
"Over there!"
Dad pointed to the east
where against the streaks of rainy dawn
he spied the only gray dot
whose movement was unnatural
for a bird.
"It's him!"
My voice cracked in excitement.
"He said he'd come!"
I yelled, running toward the house.
"Mom! It's Thomas! Mom!"
Mom came to the door, spoon in hand,
opened the screen.
"What on earth . . . ?"
I jumped in the air.
"Mom, it's Thomas! Look—
he's coming over!"
Mom hurried out to the yard,

frowning at the sky
till she saw it,
and we all stood in the drizzle
as the plane grew larger
and the drone became
a steady roar.
Then it was on us,
low and terrible,
a B-24 bomber.
Five times it circled
while I shouted
and jumped and pointed.
Mom, quiet,
shook her head.
We watched the wings tip hello.
We saw the landing gear lower, then retract.
We saw the insignia.
We saw the guns.
With one last salute from the wings,
the bomber turned,
lumbered off
the way it had come,
till the only sound
was the patter of rain
on dust
and the lowing of an impatient cow
from the barn.
At that moment, watching the gray
of Thomas's plane
disappear into the gray of the dawn,
I would have given anything,

anything,
to be up there, too.
Looking at Mom, though,
gripping that spoon,
I figured it best
not to say.

July 1943
For Annylee

One hot morning,
I should have been cutting oats,
but Mom asked me to help pick apricots.
Dad said just to come on out
when I was done.
We were under the tree
when Charles Darney's old Studebaker
churned past.
"Goin' to the graveyard," Mom said.
The basket was about full
when we heard the shotgun
from the top of the hill.
"Oh, Lord—"
Mom took off her apron.
"We'd better get up there.
I'll fetch the car."
We had to slow down on the winding lanes,
but soon we could see Charles,
still standing.
He watched us pull up.

Mom leaned out the window.
"Charles, we heard the shotgun—
we were worried!"
Looking sheepish
and annoyed at the same time,
he spat.
"Sorry for yer trouble, May.
It's them gol-danged gophers!
Got me riled.
I come to blast 'em out
once't and for all."
We got out and leaned against the car
while Charles talked.
He leaned his shotgun
against the tree
and paced.
I bet he spoke more words
in that half hour
than in the last year
all told.
"My Annylee—
she were so deservin'," he said,
"jus' makes my blood boil
seein' her grave tore up!"
He choked on the words
but once he got started,
couldn't seem to stop.
"And here's what I can't get outta
my mind:
I never give her nothin'.
Y' could claim it was 'cause

she didn't live long enough—
that I woulda in time—
but truth is,
I might never.
I took her for granted.
She wore herself out
workin' for me and the boy
and I never give her nothin'.
Never told her . . .
what she'd a liked to hear.
I put bread on the table ever' day—
that were my way of sayin'.
I never raised a hand in anger.
I done what she asked
in the way of chores.
But I guess it ain't the same
as saying
what they like to hear.
Now—
it's too late."
"Charles, it's not true," Mom said.
"You gave Annylee everything!"
Charles spat and considered this.
"Well, ye know, May,
I lied when I said I never give 'er
nothing.
Christmas afore she passed
I give 'er a new dress.
I never done that before—
she always sewed up her own.
Don't know what got into me.

I's passin' the Woolworth's,
seen a dummy in the window
in a dress so purty
made me think of Anny,
how nice she'd look
dressed up like that.
Can't even tell ye what color it were.
All kinds, I guess,
with flowers.
I went in there and looked around,
finally found the rack
where that dress were hanging
in umpteen differ'nt sizes.
Lucky for me,
that ol' busybody Effie Thompson
saw me and come on in,
figured she knew which one would fit
Annylee.
When I give the box to Anny
she looked like she been snakebit,
she were so surprised.
And when she took out that dress,
held it up,
she like to cried,
she were that pleased.
She never did put it on—
just put it box and all
under the bed.
Said she'd save it
for somethin'"—
he covered his eyes with one hand—

"somethin' special."
He pointed toward the grave.
"I buried her in that dress,
still brand new,
right out of the box.
And them damn gophers—!"
At this, he choked up again.
Mom reached out,
put a hand on Charles's sleeve.
"Charles, think now.
Anny knew you cared.
Look how you're out here
all the time,
still taking care of her.
She knows.
I'm sure of it."
He nodded at the ground,
took out a hankie, blew his nose.
Mom started to get back in the car
but turned once more to Charles.
"You and Curtis Ray
come on out to supper on Sunday.
We'll talk some more."
Charles shook his head.
"May, that's kindly of ye," he said,
"but ain't no more talkin' to it."
He stood up,
fetched his shotgun
from against the tree,
touched his cap,
and trudged away to his car.

From There Acrost

When Cyrus LeBeau brought the mail
it was generally about nine
and already hot.
We would hear the engine
whining up the hill
as he went down through every gear
of his 1932 Dodge.
Sometimes he ground on by
without stopping,
just tapping the horn hello.
But Mom always went to the window,
and if Cyrus stopped
she didn't have to tell me to go
see what had come.
Today I ran
all the way back up the drive
yelling, "Postcard, Mom!
We got a postcard!"
"Dear Folks,
I'm in Walla Walla, Washington State—
beautiful country,
as you can see on the other side of this.
We're all itching to get started acrost
the Pacific,
so this waiting is the hardest part.
I feel ready and eager.
We have a big job to do—
but we're all game.

I don't know how the mail will be
from now on,
so please don't worry
if you don't hear.
I love you all.
Yours,
Thomas."

September 1943
The Camp

We went to grind the end of last year's corn
out toward Fiatt.
Dad, me, Stinky.
We pulled up beside the elevator.
"Looks like there's a wait."
Ahead the Burtons' truck was idling,
not moving on in.
It was hot,
even hotter in the truck,
and the window on my side
wouldn't roll down.
Stinky flopped around,
fanned his face with his hand.
"Can we get out?" he said. "Walk back
along the crick?"
Dad nodded, so Stinky and I hopped out,
scampered down into the ditch,
and hiked along
through the tall weeds,

bees rumbling around the brown-eyed Susans,
heat pushing from all sides.
Stinky pointed. "There's the crick."
We climbed out of the ditch and set off
across a field of stubble,
hot as a griddle in the sun,
toward the shade trees ahead.
I was too hot to talk,
but not Stinky.
"And Curtis Ray told me
he can smoke a cigarette backwards—
y'know, lit end in—
and blow the smoke out his ears."
In the trees, it was some cooler.
Wading in the creek would be better.
If it was full
we could take a dip.
Suddenly I stopped,
put an arm out to shut Stinky up.
"Shh," I whispered. "Someone's there."
We squinted through the shady gloom
at a shack,
a horse tied to a tree,
a man, his back to us,
washing something in a basin.
I remembered what Grama'd said
about the camp on the road to Fiatt.
"A gypsy," I whispered.
We moved back into the brush,
not taking our eyes off the man
in case we missed our chance

to witness him
begging or thieving.
He was washing clothes,
hanging them on a line.
I motioned to Stinky to follow.
The man dumped out the water
and under cover of the splashing
we slipped among the trees
till we were only a few yards away.
He left the basin upside down on a stump
and turned to go inside.
We crept on.
There were other little houses.
A woman sat near a fire
stirring something in a pot.
Children played in the dirt,
leaned on their mothers.
Men sat whittling. One chopped wood.
At the end of the village
outside the last shack
I saw Jozef
in his undershirt,
carrying wood.
In the library, in his jacket and spectacles,
he looked old,
but here
he looked strong.
I noticed for the first time
he didn't walk like an old man.
He disappeared around the corner of the shack.
Stinky and I looked at each other.

Crouching, we circled the shack,
surprised
there weren't any windows,
so we leaned our foreheads against the boards
to peer through the cracks.
But before I could adjust to the dark inside
someone gripped my collar,
hauled me back a step.
"And what we find?"
Stinky and I squirmed,
unable to free ourselves
from Jozef's firm grip,
then gave up,
hanging our heads.
"I'm sorry, sir," I started. "We just—"
"You want to see," he finished. We nodded.
"Then come."
He gestured toward the shack.
Inside it was dark and hot
but Jozef slid a wooden bar along one wall
and pushed.
A large square of wall tipped out and up.
He did the same on the other side.
A toasted breeze moved through
and now we could see
a cot, a table, two chairs,
a cupboard carved and painted
with birds and flowers.
"Welcome," said Jozef.
"We're really sorry," I said.
"We didn't know your place was here.

We were walking home
from the elevator."
I looked around.
"Is this like your house in Polska?" I asked,
showing off my Polish for Stinky.
"Ya, is very like," Jozef answered.
He went to the cupboard, opened one of the doors,
and took out a small metal ball,
size of a pullet egg.
"From Nowy Targ. Is button," he explained.
"I make. Silver."
"Wow!" Stinky took a look,
handed it to me. "You made it?"
He nodded. "Beautiful clothings there.
Beautiful buttons."
I whistled, hefting the button.
It was light, hollow.
"*Real* silver?" I asked, handing it back.
"Of course real," said Jozef.
He held it up, looked it over
and set it on a saucer on the shelf.
Next he slid open a drawer and took out a photo,
creased and worn.
A young man gazed solemnly,
his bulky woolen coat adorned
with two rows of the bulbous buttons.
I studied the face. "Is this your son?"
Jozef took back the photo,
smiled, held it up
beside his face. "Is me!"
"I have thirty years then," he explained.

"Do you have a picture of your son?" I asked.
Jozef took another photo from the drawer,
this one almost crumbling.
We didn't touch it.
The same young man was standing
with a young woman
nearly buried in all her clothes—
a broad skirt, more than one shawl,
several necklaces of large silver disks.
On the woman's lap,
a baby.
"My wife, Aniela," said Jozef,
"and my son, Antoni.
He is man now,
sixteen years."
The baby's fierce eyes
looked straight at me.
I wondered if Jozef knew
what newspapers said
about Poland,
about Nazis exterminating
hundreds of thousands.
I thought I should tell him,
but looking at the boy who was sixteen,
I didn't want to.
"They live in a village
away from the city,
right?" I asked instead.
Jozef nodded.
"When did you see them last?"
Jozef turned to put the photo back

and stood with his back to us,
not answering.
Finally he turned to us.
"Is many years," he said.
"Why did you leave Poland?"
Jozef hesitated, glancing at Stinky.
"Am very sorry," he said simply.
He stood up and went to the door.
"I work very much now."

September 1943
Sparrows

A cool night, a Sunday,
I wasn't sleeping.
Something inside my chest
was roiling,
fluttering.
I thought of the B-24
flying over the Pacific toward Japan,
thousands of feet up,
the ocean below,
and Thomas in it.
I sat up and leaned into the window,
forehead against the screen,
breathing the damp, earthy air,
listening to the night rustles and hoots.
I slipped from bed, found pants, shoes,
pulled on a sweater,
let myself out,

quiet.
In the barn, I grabbed a feed sack from a nail,
climbed the ladder to the loft.
No need for light—
I knew the way by feel;
light would only startle
the sparrows.
I straddled the eight-by-eight beam
angled toward the roof,
inching my way up.
When I got to the crossbeam, I paused
while my eyes focused
in the dark.
There they were:
half a dozen sleeping spatzies,
close enough to touch.
With one arm
I swept the birds into the bag.
Dumb things
never knew what hit 'em—
except for one, the one farthest from me,
which woke in time
and with a frenzied whipping of wings
dived off the beam,
landing a few yards away.
It sidestepped,
cocking a nervous eye at me.
I cast about for something to throw,
thought of the big hay rope.
I backed down the beam, reached out,
hurled it toward the bird,

then soon as it swung back
chucked it again.
Airborne, the sparrow swooped and veered
in panic
as the rope arced around the barn.
I gave the rope a shove every time it passed.
Finally, exhausted and confused,
the bird lit on the beam
two feet away.
I took a swipe
and it was in my hand.
Startled, I almost dropped it
but managed to hold on,
caging it with my hand against my chest,
its little wings beating insanely
in its prison
while I sat,
feed sack in one hand,
bird in the other.
There must have been five or six birds in the bag;
I'd have the most at school tomorrow.
The bird in my hand, warm,
stopped fighting.
I imagined the tiny patter
of its heart,
and for some reason
instead of tossing it in the bag,
I waited,
sitting on the beam.

Dear Thomas

Dear Thomas,
I don't know if they tell you
what's happening in Europe.
We're bombing Berlin
big time.
Gabe's in Florida now
for amphibious training.
I guess you know what that is.
Janie says it won't be long
till he goes overseas.
Curtis Ray got took home by the sheriff last week.
He was out the London Mills road
in his dad's car
and went in a ditch.
He told me Charles beat him good
and gave him three weeks
to get a job
and move out.
Yesterday at school we typed to music.
I'd be doing 16 W.P.M. (words per minute)
if I could keep up.
Sarah Mulberry is at 25 W.P.M.
She doesn't know it,
but I'm trying to beat her.
A couple days ago Ring chased a coon up a tree
and Stinky got it by the paw with his lasso
and we caught it under a tub,
but we let it go.

So That's the News From Ellisville.
Keep 'em flying!
Eddie

December 1943
Aunt Callista

If the president really wanted to win the war,
he should put gramas
in charge.
"Eddie, not there—here!
Then clear the pantry.
Make room on the cart."
I wished there were girls
in the Carl family
instead of just Thomas and me.
And this Christmas,
just me.
I set the cookies
where she said,
then started for the
pantry cart.
I was shoving jars and bottles
into the lower shelves
when I remembered
that old tin
from years ago.
I bent down, looked for it
in the back.
There it was.

I wanted to know
if the money was still there.
But this time I didn't sneak.
I brought it out,
took it to Grama.
"Grama, I found this,"
I said.
Grama sucked in her breath,
looked sharply at me.
She wiped her hands
on her apron
and reached out
to take the tin.
"Did you look in it?"
she asked.
"Once.
When I was little," I said.
She nodded toward the table.
"Sit down."
We sat
and Grama pushed the cookie trays
to make room for the tin.
"No reason you shouldn't know,"
she said,
and took off the lid.
There was money,
but Grama laid that aside,
reached in again
and with difficulty
pulled out a stiff paper.
She looked at it

for some seconds
then laid it in front of me.
"That there's our Callista,"
she said,
keeping one finger
on the corner.
It was a photo—
a tiny girl
in a ruffled dress and bonnet,
propped up but nearly toppling
in the corner of the old davenport.
"She was born before your dad.
She . . . died.
When she was three."
I stared.
I didn't pick it up
because Grama kept her finger
on it.
The baby was so covered
in frills,
I could barely see her face,
but her sharp little eyes
looked like a Carl, all right.
"What happened?" I finally asked.
Grama waited to answer.
"You know, honey,
something I learnt
over the years is,
a story like this starts out big—
near on too long to tell.
Then in time it boils down

to just a few words.

And that's a blessing.
Forty-five years ago,
woulda took me
a week to tell this story.
But now
it comes down to
poor thing took cold and died."
"Does Dad remember?"
"No, he was just a baby.
But he knows."
I thought about Grampa Rob.
"Grampa . . ."
Grama put the photo back in the tin
with the money
and snapped the lid on.
"Your Grampa took it hard.
Nearly killed him.
That little girl was
the apple of his eye."
She paused.
"He was different then.
When little Callie passed
he thought . . .
well . . .
he thought
I shoulda minded her
better.
Maybe he was right."
She stood up and walked to the pantry,
put the tin on the shelf.

"And what about the money?
What's that for?"
She turned,
defiant.
"Thirty years, every week,
I put some aside.
Knowing it's there—
it helps."
I must have looked shocked.
"Don't you worry."
She smiled.
"I ain't going nowhere.
There's nowhere else I want to be.
Now give me that next batch."
I handed her a tray;
she opened the oven
and slid it in.

December 1943
The Race

The old Smith Corona
Dad rented for me
had some mileage on it,
but the good typewriters
had gone to the war.
It had its quirks—
the *x* and the *e* hung up now and then.
We didn't type many x's,
but the e was hard to avoid,

so one day I found some oil,
got in there under the hood,
souped things up.
Round about thirty-five words a minute
I began to get the hang of it
and Sarah began to get
nervous.
I could tell.
Every day at the end of class
was the timed drill.
At "Go!" we would start,
fourteen of us filling the room
with a mad-clacking din
for one full minute
till "Stop!"
Sarah would look at me
and I'd tell her the last words I'd typed
before she told me hers,
always
with the same sure-laughing grin.
At first it wasn't even close,
but week by week
I edged up on her.
Then at forty-nine I hit a wall:
forty-nine, forty-six, forty-eight.
Somehow my dumb mitts just couldn't pound any
faster.
Or maybe it wasn't my fingers;
maybe I just couldn't think the letters
any faster than that.
Brain or body,

Sarah was at fifty-five.
I thought forty-nine was good,
but Sarah's fingers at fifty-five W.P.M.
were a thing of beauty,
long, curved, and not so much hitting the keys
as flying, waving over them,
a witch with a spell,
not pounding or hammering,
but clickity tapping.
Sometimes during exercises,
I'd glance over
and see her typing and watching me,
typing and not even looking
at the keys,
and seeing my amazement,
she'd smile
and I would lose my place,
but God's truth,
I'd rather fail typing altogether
than stop looking at Sarah's smile
at fifty-five W.P.M.

December 1943
Basketball

Balanced on the ladder,
I took off one glove, then the other,
huffed on my hands
to warm them up,
pulled the gloves back on,

and tapped the last couple of nails
into the backboard.
I jumped down,
dragged the ladder into the barn,
trotted toward the house.
"Dad—it's ready! Come on!" I yelled,
taking the steps two at a time.
Inside, Dad buckled his boots.
"Come on, Dad. You got the ball?"
In reply he scooped the ball with one hand,
sent it straight into my stomach.
"Oooff! Hey, you're gonna get it now!"
I grabbed the ball,
bounded back outside.
Not exactly basketball weather,
but when the big boxes had come
I'd torn them open
and there was no way I was gonna wait
for spring.
We'd read the note,
hardly believing the boxes were real:
"Bud, you'd love Hawaii—
we play basketball every chance we get.
If you're reading this
it means my pal Dale
was able to mail it
in San Diego.
Practice up, little guy,
so I can whomp you good
when I get home.
Merry Christmas—

Thomas."
We danced around the yard,
clumsy in our gloves.
We dribbled and faked and jumped,
laughing and panting,
breathing hard,
till we'd shed our gloves,
our hats and coats.
The ball crunched on the gravel,
bounced off rocks;
we lurched and missed and ran after it.
I was first to make a shot.
From ten feet,
the ball arced and plummeted
straight through the net.
"Hey!" said Dad. "Pretty fancy.
Gimme that—" and he tried,
but again and again
the ball hit the rim.
I found my rhythm: dribble, dribble, jump,
the right wrist-flip and—
swish.
Dad grabbed a rebound,
took his time,
guarded the ball,
dribbling it around the barnyard.
"Come on, Dad—you're hogging it!"
I lunged, but he blocked me.
I saw his frown
and backed off a bit,
giving him room to set up the shot.

No go.
I caught it off the rim, tossed it to him.
"You're just rusty.
Go on. I'll feed 'em to you."
He nodded and stood in front of the basket,
shot after shot,
while I chased the balls.
I was cold
but I didn't want to break his concentration
getting my coat.
Ten, twenty missed shots.
Thirty—
he would not give up.
And he didn't get mad.
Just stood there
taking the shots.
Long about forty-five,
the ball caught the rim,
circled, circled,
and tipped in.
"All right!" I yelled, jumping for my dad,
pounding him on the back.
He grinned but didn't move
from the spot.
"Gimme another one."
I tossed him the ball,
and of the next ten shots
he made six
before Mom yelled dinner.
We got our coats and headed up the drive.
"I knew you'd get it back!" I said.

Dad shook his head,
trace of a smile.
"Didn't get it back," he said.
"I never done it before."
I couldn't believe it.
"You never played basketball?"
"Nope."
He bounced the ball.
"Just one of them things—
never got the chance."
I thought about Dad never playing before.
"Well, dang," I said,
"I guess you done pretty good then!"
"Yep." Dad laughed,
clapping me on the back.
"Pretty good
for an old man."

December 1943
Just Doing My Job

Dear All,
Some excitement today—
went on my first run.
You know I can't say anything exact,
but I'll tell you this:
it was something!
My crew didn't fly—
we rode with an expert crew.
Good thing, too—
we learned some tricks they didn't teach us

in training.
I had knots in my stomach.
Some of the guys were sick.
I'm glad now
they made me a bomber.
Those fighters must feel awful alone
up there.
My crew's rarin' to go.
They're all excellent guys.
I can't believe my luck
getting such a swell bunch.
I'm going to do my best
not to let them down.
I'm glad you got help shucking.
You probably won't believe it,
but I wish I was there to help.
I miss the farm,
even the work.
Well, it's been a long day
and soon it's lights out,
but I wanted to write.
Thanks for all your letters—
they give me a real boost.
Tell Janie to write Gabe
that we're all with him
on that ship to Europe.
Merry Christmas!
I'll be thinking about you.
Love,
Thomas

December 1943
The Photograph

Christmas—
leather gloves,
graph paper, pencils, a comb,
a dollar from Aunt Pearl in Kentucky,
a book I'd been wanting: *Daniel Boone.*
Then to Grama Lucy's
for lunch
and the photograph.
Every year since Thomas was born,
two photos on Grampa's old Brownie camera
stand straight, keep still,
wipe the grin off your face,
us lined up, from Dad to me,
one snap, then another with Grama.
None with Grampa.
No one could touch that camera
but him.
"Besides," he always said,
"my face'd break the thing."
Now Grampa took coats
while we all Merry Christmas'd.
Grama yoo-hooed from the kitchen.
Mom took off her hat,
pushed her hair around.
"Picture first?" she asked.
Grampa clapped his hands. "Yes, ma'am,
right this way."
"What about Ma?" asked Dad.

"Let's get you all first," answered Grampa.
We stood Dad, Mom, me,
strange without Thomas,
Grampa behind the tripod—
straighten up, don't move, *snap*—
"We're done."
"I'll get Ma," said Dad,
but Grampa was taking down the tripod.
"No need," he said.
"She had a little run-in
with the kitchen door—
don't look too good.
Thought it best not to pose."
Dad stared,
started for the kitchen.
"Ma! What's this? Did he—"
"Wynton, don't fuss," Grama said,
coming to the door.
Half her face was blue.
"Ain't nothing—
nothing's broke. Just ran into
that dang swing door.
Won't happen again."
Dad looked at Grampa,
his voice strange.
"No, Ma, it won't."
Grampa Rob leaned the tripod in a corner
and strode toward the kitchen.
Dad blocked his way.
"Right, Pa?"
"Time to eat!" Grampa said.

Dad didn't move
and Grampa stood there
with his jaw out.
"Wyn"—Mom put her hand
on Dad's shoulder—
"it's Christmas.
Please."
Dad hesitated,
looked at Grama,
stood aside.
Grampa brushed on past.

February 1944
The Fire

Sunday afternoons in winter,
we played Chinese checkers,
though Dad said there wasn't much point,
since Mom always won.
We were putting things away
when the phone rang,
three short rings.
Dad was nearest and lifted the receiver.
I heard the faint, high-pitched whine
of the person on the other end,
saw the startled look
on Dad's face.
"Strothers' is on fire," he told us.
"Oh, mercy," breathed Mom,
"we better all go."

I got my coat and boots on.
"I'll get buckets!" I offered
and raced outside.
The blast of icy air made me suck in my breath
and I slipped and slid
on the frozen ground.
When I turned from the milk house
I saw the sky.
The Strothers were half a mile north
and sure enough
smoke was curling up.
I thought of Lem and Laura
getting on in years,
third generation in that house,
them with all their cats,
their boy Leo
off working in Chicago.
When we got close enough in the car
we could see it was the shed
a few yards from the house.
With the wind,
the fire could jump.
Lem and half a dozen men
passed buckets from the pump.
Grampa Rob was there yelling orders
while women carried clothes and china
out of the house.
Laura came out, cat in one arm,
feed bag full of something in the other.
"May, I can't find Feisty!" she yelled.
The cat in her arms

launched itself, sprinted for the barn
as Laura threw the sack on a pile
in the yard
and headed back up the steps,
Mom behind her.
The shed was in full blaze.
I helped the men.
The path from the pump to the shed
was slick
so we handed the buckets in a line
instead of running.
Every time we passed a bucket
the splashes crackled into ice
till our clothes and faces were frosted
even in the heat.
"Get back—it's going!" Grampa yelled.
"Oh, Lord!" someone cried. "There it goes!"
The shed buckled and leaned.
Sheets of blackened, curling tar paper
tossed straight up,
floated in the wind toward the house.
"We're gone," cried Lem,
pointing at the roof
and backing away
as the shed walls caved.
The house caught in no time.
We threw down our buckets,
but Grampa wasn't done.
"Save the furniture!" he yelled
and charged into the house.
Twenty minutes later we all stood in the yard,

driven out by smoke and danger,
and watched
as the fire did its job.
Lem and Laura stood sagging
next to the pile
of what we'd saved,
all of us wanting to do more,
but helpless.
Another hour and the house was gone.
It burnt to the ground
while we helped Lem and Laura
carry their belongings to the barn.
Bedsteads and tables, the hall tree,
Laura's antique rocker,
books and dishes and the family Bible.
Four men carried the big walnut wardrobe,
all the clothes still inside.
Grampa kept bossing
and in the end the barn was set up
neat as a bungalow.
He said to Laura, "See there?
If ya had you some heat
you could move right in."
Laura looked all around
and burst out crying.
The women put their arms around her,
but she still couldn't stop.

February 1944
The Hero

Potluck at the Fairgates',
and the big deal
is Deylon Reevy
in uniform,
all buttons and brass,
pleats and pockets.
He's only a private,
not a single stripe,
but the girls all hang and coo,
"Hey, Deylon!"
The boys stand back,
hide their stares.
Some hero.
Just last month
he was dumb as a fence post.

May 1944
The Accusation

Curtis Ray's desk at Hindeman's Insurance
is older than anyone knows.
You'd need a pitchfork
to dig through the mess of
scribbled notes, ashtrays, rubber bands,
into the ink spills and coffee stains,
and on down through the brown paint
into the good old oak.

It was built to be sturdy,
all tongued and grooved.
If someone peeled and scraped and sanded,
that desk would be
quite a prize.
I had plenty of time to study it
when I stopped by on instructions from Mom
to invite Charles Darney and Curtis Ray
to Sunday dinner.
They wouldn't come—
she'd been asking ever since that day
in the graveyard—
but Mom said to ask anyways.
"Mr. Darney isn't in,"
Agnes Strother said when I walked in.
"But if you'd like to wait,
he's on a call and will be back soon."
Ha. Mr. Darney.
Curtis Ray wasn't even a salesman.
His job was to drum up business
for the real salesmen.
And that meant ringing doorbells,
since most folks in Ellisville
didn't have phones.
Still, he wore a shirt and tie,
had a desk,
and they must have been paying him,
'cause he was renting a room
in town.
I sat staring at the desk
till he hustled in.

I stood up and put out my hand.
"Mr. Darney!" I said
in my deepest voice.
He ignored my hand,
straightened his tie as he sat down.
As we talked
he played with a pencil,
glancing around at the men at the other desks.
He said he'd check about Sunday.
I told him Dad had a new idea
for getting rid of the gophers.
Then abruptly he stood,
motioning me to follow him outside.
On the sidewalk, he said,
"I didn't want Agnes to hear.
Hey, Eddie—you were at Strothers'
the night it burned, right?"
I nodded.
"I was just over to see them," he said.
"They ain't insured
and Mr. Hindeman thought maybe, well—
'once burned' and all—
maybe they'd be interested,
now they hafta rebuild."
"Yeah?" I asked, wondering what the big deal was.
"So I'm talking to Lem and Laura
and they ask me
does fire insurance cover *arson*."
I swallowed.
"Arson? They think someone set the fire
on purpose?"

"Or by accident," Curt answered.
"They think someone was in there
maybe trying to get warm."
"Why would someone go there
to get warm?"
Curtis Ray looked impatient.
"They didn't *go* there to get warm.
They went there for something else.
Got cold waiting."
"Did Lem and Laura see someone?"
Curtis Ray shook his head.
"Found something, though," he said.
"I'm supposed to show Mr. Hindeman,
then give it to the sheriff."
He put a hand in his pocket, palmed something.
Then, holding his hand near his side
so nobody but me could see,
he opened his fist.
The soot-covered object was small and round,
about the size of a pullet egg.
Jozef's silver button.

May 1944
The Button

When Curt showed me the button
I should have told him what it was,
but I didn't.
I just stood there
looking at it.

"Uh—what is it?" I said.

"Dunno," he said, pocketing the button again.

"Looks like silver."

I knew Jozef hadn't left it there.

I wasn't so sure about others in the camp.

I wondered if Jozef had noticed

it was gone.

Or maybe it wasn't his.

Maybe lots of gypsies

had buttons like that.

The next Saturday, I saddled Hettie,

took her out the Fiatt road.

The creek was full and rushing

at the north end of the camp.

I had to walk Hettie half a mile south

to get across,

then back along the path

between the creek and the camp.

It was hard not to be seen

up top of Hettie.

People stopped what they were doing.

Children ran inside

to get their moms and dads,

who stood in doorways,

staring as I passed.

Near Jozef's

two men walked through the trees,

blocked my path.

The first took hold of Hettie's harness.

She jerked her head.

He whispered,

and she was still.

"Hello, friend," said the other man,
looking me over.
"You visit us today?"
"I, uh—yes," I said,
"I'm here to see Jozef Mirga."
The two exchanged looks.
"You are boy . . . from library," said the first man,
still holding onto Hettie.
I nodded.
He shrugged and let go
and they both stepped back.
I nudged Hettie on,
felt their eyes on my back
as we plodded past.
Jozef was outside, shaving.
A little mirror
hung on the side of his house.
There was a fire in the pit
heating water.
"Eddie Carl!" he said,
wiping his face with a towel.
"You are surprising me!"
I slid down off Hettie.
"Jozef," I said,
getting right to the point,
"have you lost your silver button?"
The man looked puzzled.
"No. Why?"
"Could you look?
Somebody found one."

Jozef beckoned me into the house,
went to the cupboard,
opened the little door.
His amazement seemed genuine
when there was nothing there.
"What—"
He opened other doors and drawers
then turned to me
for the answer.
"You know Lem and Laura Strother—
how their place burned?"
Jozef nodded. "Yes," he said.
"Well, they're getting ready to rebuild,
and they found a button
in the ashes.
Curtis Ray Darney has it;
he's gonna give it to the sheriff."
Jozef sat down,
motioning me to the other chair.
He sighed.
"This sheriff—
is good man?"
"I guess so," I said. I'd never really
thought about it.
"Then we not worry.
I do no wrong."
"But Jozef, what if . . ."
Jozef showed me to the door.
"Eddie, you are good friend.
I thank you."

The Goof

I was eating an ice cream bar
at the Rural Youth picnic in Canton Park,
watching some of the others
at the ring toss
and I was thinking about
eating another one
when Sarah sat on the ground
beside me.
She had an ice cream bar, too.
"Hey, Eddie," she said,
"what's new with you?"
I guess I was nervous,
having her there so close
asking me what's new,
or maybe I just had so much
on my mind,
I felt like talking,
but before I knew it
I'd told her all about
Jozef, Aniela, Antoni,
and the button.
She was quiet a minute,
then said, "I don't think he did it."
"What? How do you know?"
"Because I know him some,"
she answered. "He shoes
for us sometimes. He just
wouldn't do it,

that's all."
She finished her ice cream
and dug in the dirt
with the stick.
"Hey, Eddie,
you going to the new picture at the Capitol?
Wild Bill Elliott is in it."
I said, "You bet—*Mojave Firebrand.*
I saw the posters."
"Me, too!" she said.
We sat for a minute,
me not knowing what to say,
till she got up and said,
"Well, see you in school,"
and I said, "Okay,"
and she walked away.
It hit me then:
I could have asked her to the movie
with me.
But she might have said no,
and anyway,
I'd missed my chance.
I thought what a stupid goof I was
and wondered what
she thought.

Dear Thomas

Dear Thomas,
Got 4 letters from you yesterday—
got to read about your 4 missions
and your 50 combat hours.
I wish you could tell more.
The newspapers give plenty of numbers,
but I want to know what it's really like,
flying a mission.
Here, it's the same as always—
putting up hay, cutting mullen.
Mom and Janie are always bragging
about their boys in uniform.
Janie says Gabe's in England,
commando training.
They're glad he's not a paratrooper.
I read those guys are jumping
by the thousands.
Seems like he'll never get to fighting,
but they think soon.
Dopey Deylon Reevy joined up.
He seems to get home most weekends.
Walks around in his uniform
and salutes the old guys
from the first war.
Walter Fairgate saw me in town and said
say hello to the hero,
so I told him sure,
I'd write to Gabe real soon.

(Ha ha—just kidding.)
Give 'em heck, hero.
Eddie

June 1944
The Dream

Usually I sleep so hard,
I don't even dream.
Or if I do,
I don't remember.
When I wake up
I don't know where I am.
I've had a few dreams, though,
and I'll never forget this one.
Later I learned Gabe's mom
had been here.
I must have heard them in my sleep
and that's why I dreamed
what I did.
It was so real,
it was like I was there.
It was like I was Gabe
marching up the road with my outfit,
stomach churning,
but I held my rifle ready.
This is it, I thought.
I couldn't form any other thoughts,
just kept marching,
did what I had to do.

This is it.
This is it.
Then shots and shouts
and we were running,
shooting.
I looked ahead but didn't see anything.
Everyone ran faster.
I didn't know why.
Men around me kept stopping,
but I couldn't see why
so I ran on, clutching that rifle,
knowing I should do something,
shoot something,
but then
there was a soldier with a gun
right in front of me
and I only had one second,
just one second,
to think my last thought,
and it was just
wait a minute—
wait—
When I woke up
I could hear Mom in the kitchen
crying.
I pulled on my pants,
creaked in my bare feet across the wooden floor.
When she heard me, she turned
and at first just stood there
looking at me like I'd got up
from the dead.

Then she rushed across the room,
grabbed hold,
held on tight
and could hardly talk for crying.
"Gabe's gone," she told me,
"killed at Normandy."

June 1944
For Gabe

The second hardest thing, Mom said,
was writing to Thomas.
The hardest
was being with Janie.
Friends from the time they were girls,
like sisters.
Hard as it was, though,
everyone was proud.
The ultimate sacrifice, they said.
Janie and Jack put the gold star
in their window
and in town I saw men grip Jack's hand,
pat his shoulder.
"You can be proud of that boy, Jack.
We're all proud."
Me, I couldn't take it in.
I'd forget it for a minute
and then it would come back, hard,
a punch to the gut—
Gabe dead, killed,

never coming back,
never coming home.
What did he say
the day we threw the cobs . . .
I told him don't listen to me—
but then I remembered all my big talk.
What did I know?
Of all the guys,
Gabe was first to decide.
He went because he thought it was right.
He went and fought
and got killed
and here I was alive and whole
and still shooting my mouth
like I knew something
when I didn't.
Gabe,
who never told me to get lost,
never coming home.
Most of the time
it didn't seem real.
Then one day in the calf pasture cutting mullen
it hit me again
and wouldn't turn loose—
wave after wave, right to the gut.
I heaved up my breakfast
and started to cry.
Why, Gabe?
Why'd you go?
Why didn't you stay here
safe?

I knew why he went,
but why'd it have to be him
that got killed?
And Thomas—
I wanted him back.
No more missions,
no more combat hours.
I heaved again,
hardly able to think *what if*—
what if Thomas
didn't make it back.
He had to.
It couldn't happen that both of them
would die,
their mothers like sisters,
two friends,
clear across the world from each other,
both dying in the war.
It couldn't happen.

July 1944
In the Barn

We baled hay like devils all week,
Dad and me, Grampa Rob, and Dawsons—
738 bales on the best day.
Then, putting up the last load,
the loader broke.
While Dad and Dale fixed it,
Stinky and I debated what to do.

"Let's sit in the horse-barn loft," I said.
But Stinky was thirsty.
"I'm going for lemonade," he said
and headed toward the house.
The sun was hot on the gravel,
hot reflecting off the barn.
I went in the little side-pen door,
hoping for cool,
but a closed barn in July
is just shelter from the sun,
the air still and close.
I was thinking lemonade at the house
sounded better
when I heard something
and stopped there in the pen,
listening.
Grampa, in the filtered light
by Beauty's stall,
sagged, looking old.
I stood quiet.
He was putting away tack
in the box.
Then the straw crackled
under my foot
and Grampa turned.
I could have hid,
but I didn't.
I stepped out,
stood there looking.
"Damn it, boy!"
He lifted his jaw,

started toward me,
barking, "How long you been there
spyin'?"
I didn't know what he meant,
why it was spying.
"Awhile," I exaggerated
and stood my ground.
He spat.
"You get on back.
See if that loader's fixed."
I shrugged and left,
but after supper,
the others drinking iced tea,
I had a chance.
I went to the tack box
and lifted the lid.
In a corner
under brushes and bits and halter hooks,
was a metal box,
small,
inside it
a ribbon,
a wooden block,
and a doll—
a cornhusk doll—
and stitched on its apron, one word,
"Callista."

The Barbershop

Hank Gillum took his time
snipping Walter Fairgate's few remaining hairs.
Hank couldn't talk and snip
at the same time
so he'd yammer a while, then snip,
then yammer some more.
Hank was big,
with a big voice,
big opinions,
and a haircut usually took awhile.
He wasn't in any hurry.
He was on about the new bank alarm,
how Myrtle Putnam
told so many people how it works,
anyone wanting to rob the place
could just walk in there
and push the Off button.
Hank's laugh,
a squealy little snort,
starts small
and gets louder and louder
till it's like a goose honk.
It's even funnier than whatever story
he's telling,
so everyone was laughing.
Even Charles Darney, in the corner,
cracked a smile.
I picked up a *Life* magazine

and settled in.
I liked to look at *Life*,
especially stories about the war
with pictures.
I always looked for Thomas.
This time it was B-24s
on a field in the Aleutians
just before a raid,
crew standing around
in leather jackets
looking at a big dark sky,
probably wondering
if they'd come back that night.
In another picture they were lowering
a wounded guy
through the bomb hatch
onto a stretcher.
I couldn't see his face.
Even the ads were about the war.
In one painting, bombers flew
practically up in space,
the Earth below
just a small blue globe
with big orange bomb blasts
in Europe and Japan.
I wanted to ask Hank for that page
to put it up at home,
but I'd always been a little afraid of him.
I glanced up,
thinking I might ask
and saw that no one was laughing.

They were talking about the fire,
about the silver button.
They'd heard talk about gypsies
out the Fiatt road
having buttons like that.
I pretended to keep reading.
Oscar Keal was pretty het up:
"The Strothers coulda died,"
he said. "That's akin to murder."
Oscar was kind of excitable.
You never knew what he'd say next.
Charles Darney was digging his pipe
in his tobacco pouch.
Walter objected. "Well, that's not right, Oscar.
There has to be *intention* to murder
for it to be murder.
Fact is, nobody died."
Hank jabbed the air with his shears
as he talked.
"To hell with intentions!" he boomed.
"That weren't nobody with no
friendly intentions,
no matter what come of it."
He made one snip at Walter's sideburns,
then pointed the shears at Oscar.
"You hit the nail on the head, Oscar," he said.
"And there's plenty think so.
Sheriff ain't done nothing.
An elected official's
s'posed to act on behalf of the citizenry.
He don't act,

folks might decide
to do it for him."
Oscar and Walter were staring at him.
I was, too, and Oscar noticed me.
"Hey, Eddie," he said,
"you're friendly with that gypsy.
What you know about them
out toward Fiatt?"
I didn't know what to say.
Everyone was looking at me.
"I know him from the library,"
I finally said.
"That's all."

August 1944
The Choice

It was just a movie, I told myself.
Maybe a soda after.
Stinky and I'd done that
a hundred times.
Going with Sarah
didn't make it any different.
Ha!
I grinned like a goof into the mirror
thinking of all the ways
Sarah Mulberry
was different from Stinky Dawson.
"Eddie!" Mom called from the living room.
"Are you going or not?

You don't want to keep her waiting!"
I put the cap on the Brylcreem
and checked my hair
one more time.
I managed to get out of the house
without too much inspection
or lecturing.
Dad passed me a dollar on my way out.
"Better get some gas," he said,
"and be careful in the car, okay?"
I nodded my thanks.
Driving down the hill, I thought about
how it happened,
how I'd wanted to ask her
but couldn't find the right time
or right words,
and how in the end
she practically did it for me.
At the five-and-dime
buying pencils and paper for school,
Sarah was there, too,
and I said, "One more weekend
till school,"
and she said, "Yeah, we should do
something special,"
and after only a couple stupid seconds,
I said, "I'll probably go to the movies—
wanna come?
I could maybe get the car,"
and she smiled
and said, "Sure!"

Just outside Ellisville
I pulled into Charles Darney's filling station.
I knew how to pump gas
and Charles always let me do it,
but I didn't want to get smelly,
so I waited for him.
He came out,
put his hands on the window frame.
"Hey, Eddie. Fill 'er up?"
I nodded.
He took off the gas cap, started the pump.
I didn't expect him to talk,
but he did.
"Eddie, you's friendly with that feller Mirga,
ain't that right?"
"I guess so. What about him?"
"You think he coulda started that fire
over t' the Strothers'?"
"No. Who's saying that?"
"Oh, those guys Hank and Oscar.
They come by earlier
with Big Buss Burton
drinkin', sayin' as to how them gypsies
burnt out the Strothers."
Charles put the cap back on the gas tank,
wiped his hands on a rag he carried
in his back pocket.
"They was on about it,
sayin' it were 'cause of them
gypsies 'n' Jews
Hitler had tuh war,

so it were 'cause of them
Gabe got hisself killed."
"That's crazy," I said.
"Eighty cents."
I paid him and pulled away.
As I neared the turnoff to the Fiatt road
I thought about Jozef,
wondered if I should warn him
of what folks were saying.
But then I thought about Sarah
waiting in Ellisville,
and I drove on.

August 1944
The Date

By the time we finished our root beer
Sarah knew more about me
than maybe anyone else
in the world.
Around girls
I wasn't much of a talker,
but Sarah had a way
of getting me going.
I'd just told her
about walking the Spoon
as we slurped the last slurps.
"Golly," she said.
We sat not talking
for a minute.

"Eddie," she said suddenly,
all breathless,
"take me there!"
"Where?" I said.
"To the Spoon. I want to see!
I want to see exactly
where you walk it."
I wasn't that keen,
but you couldn't say no to Sarah
without a lot of fuss,
and I thought of the river
and the moonlight,
just us.
So I paid the bill
and we headed out the county road.
I knew exactly where.
I pulled onto the shoulder
and we walked in the hot night
through the tall grass,
crickets and frogs noisy,
to the river.
We heard it first,
not high and fast, but slow,
then saw it,
full, black,
under a wide stripe of moon.
"It was here," I said, stopping.
We stood watching,
listening.
"You were really scared,"
she observed.

"Yep," I said.

"Come on," Sarah said,
and to my shock,
she unhooked her skirt
and started on the buttons of her blouse.
"Sarah—" I started,
but she was already wading in.
"Eddie, come on!
You've been seeing me in my swimming suit
since we were born.
It's no different."
I swallowed,
thinking it was some different,
but she was up to her knees,
so I peeled off my pants and shirt
and started after.
When the water was waist high
Sarah said, "I think you should walk it."
I looked across.
It wasn't as far as I remembered.
Sarah stood in the moonlight,
looking up at me,
waiting.
"I need a rock," I said.
"No, you don't—"
She moved behind me and said,
"Get down."
I crouched,
and she waded onto my shoulders,
her hands on my head,
her long wet legs hooked under

my arms.
I walked forward,
holding her legs,
still crouching,
rising as the water deepened
until only my head was above
the water.
I remembered how I'd panicked
and gulped,
so I breathed in
smooth
and went under.
Step by step, sure and easy,
warmed by the water,
by the moonlight,
I glided across the Spoon with Sarah,
feeling like I could hold my breath
till Monday.

September 1944
The Money

After school
I helped Grampa Rob
fill his silo.
I wished I could be the one
to stand inside
and level the silage
with the big fork
as it blew in from the cutter.

But Dad said no,
too dangerous.
Just last year
two boys name of Varney
over Delavan way,
brothers,
got sucked in,
suffocated,
probably fooling around
the way kids do.
So I carried stalks
to the cutter
and fed them in
as it chugged and clattered.
I watched the cut corn
arc up and into the silo,
where Grampa spread it
with the fork.
When it got too dark to see,
Grampa yelled to turn off
the machine.
In the quiet
I was suddenly hungry.
Grama would be getting dinner.
We fit the door back on the silo.
"I'm beat," said Grampa.
I said, "You go on."
I pulled the cutter across the yard
into the tractor shed,
took a few minutes
to clean off the blades,

then headed up the drive.
Near the house,
windows were open.
Something crashed—
a dish?—
and I heard Grama cry out.
I ran,
took the stairs
in one leap,
banged through the door,
through to the kitchen.
Grampa, face twisted,
the tin on the floor,
money everywhere,
had Grama
by the wrist.
I yelled, grabbed,
wrenched him away.
"Eddie!" Grama cried,
like it was my fault.
She leaned,
shaking.
I stood in front of her
while Grampa sputtered,
his disbelief, anger
plain.
He bent to pick up
the scattered bills,
stuffing them back in the tin.
"Must be hundreds in there!
Times we coulda used

that money."
I helped Grama
to a chair at the table.
She looked at Grampa
straight.
"That money's mine," she said,
"I earned it.
Took me thirty years.
Been there all this time—
'spect it woulda been
till I died.
That's all I got to say."
"It's wrong, woman!"
Grampa shook his head,
shoved past me,
sat at his end of the table
with the tin in front of him.
He leaned forward
and pointed a warning finger
at Grama.
"We'll see about this later."
He sat back,
picked up his fork and knife.
For a minute
I couldn't move.
It was like Christmas—
same thing.
It hit me then,
how many times before
there must've been,
how many more there would be,

with nobody to stand up.
"No," I said.
They looked at me
like they'd forgot
I was there.
"It's Grama's."
I took the tin off the table,
watching Grampa,
the ropey muscles in his neck.
He glared at me,
but I stared him down
till he looked at Grama
rubbing her wrist.
For a second I was afraid
she'd tell me never mind,
that it was okay.
But she looked at me,
looked at him,
and reached out for the tin.

September 1944
The Kiss

I never thought it would be like that,
and I thought about it
a lot.
I thought about Sarah's lips—
not so much her smiling lips,
but her thinking, scheming,
dreaming lips.

I'd been looking at those
lips
for as long as I knew.
On Saturday we had a plan—
hotdogs at the Frosty Foam,
a movie at the Capitol.
I should wait,
kiss her in the dark.
But that afternoon, running errands in town,
I couldn't wait another hour.
I wanted to talk,
tell her everything.
I headed for her street,
thought I'd swing by,
cool, cruising,
her on the porch, me idling—
"Hey, let's go for a spin."
Dad would kill me
for wasting the treads—
we were running on bald,
on a waiting list for rationed tires—
but I didn't care.
I didn't think I could live anyways
till six o'clock
if I couldn't see Sarah
and those lips.
But on her street in front of her house
a car was already there
idling
and Sarah was there,
leaning toward the driver,

leaning way in,
leaning with her lips,
leaning
into Deylon Reevy's car.

September 1944
The Reject

Curtis Ray was drunk.
I hadn't seen that many drunks,
especially in the afternoon.
It was Saturday
and I was at the movies with Stinky,
since Sarah had found
other interests.
She said she didn't care for Deylon
and that I was making
a big deal
out of nothing.
But to me it wasn't nothing
when someone's launched halfway
into someone else's car
and they laugh
and say "Oh, Eddie,
don't be silly,"
and laugh
when you drive away
mad.
Anyways, I sure didn't want to see them
at the movies Saturday nights,

so I stuck to the afternoons.
Curtis Ray was there,
drunk,
and when we came out of the movie
he was behind us,
loud,
slurring like Daffy Duck,
repeating the lines
of the cartoon we'd just seen.
"Insulting myyyyyyyy in-*teg*-rity, eh?"
He stumbled forward,
gave me a little shove.
"Eh? We meet . . . on the field . . .
of honor!
No—
we meeeeet on the field of . . .
onion!"
I stopped, turned around. "Cut it out, Curt."
He appeared to consider this.
"You'rrrrre *right*, little Eddie.
Little Eddie . . . my big,
little man."
He put his hands on my shoulders.
"You'rrrr rrright.
We *cannot* meet on the field of . . . onion . . .
because . . .
Doc Gordon says I can't."
He leaned on me
and I grabbed him to keep us both
from falling.
"*You* could fight the onion, Eddie!

But not me.
Not one little . . .
onion."
He started to snivel.
Stinky and I stood there holding him up,
looking around
to see if people were watching.
We took him to his place,
Myrtle Putnam's spare room,
hauling him up the back stairs,
him blubbering most of the way.
The room was small
and smelled.
We dumped Curtis on the bed,
where he curled in a ball
and went to sleep.
"Geez, look at this," Stinky said.
It was a mess.
At the table,
he'd been writing—
scraps of paper were wadded up,
torn.
I said, "We should go,"
and headed for the door.
On the way out,
Stinky kicked a ball of paper,
then grabbed it up.
"Hey, listen," he said,
as we clumped down the stairs.
"Says, Hey, Tom—
how's the ace?"

The Telegram

I lay on the bed
staring
at the ceiling, the walls,
the air corps pennant above
Thomas's desk,
thinking about Sarah
with dopey Deylon.
Mom was in the kitchen,
rattling pans for supper.
Dad was in the living room,
warming up the radio,
when we heard a car on the hill,
heard it turn in—
unusual,
this time on a Saturday.
I rolled off the bed.
Dad was at the door,
opening it.
Mom, behind him,
gasped.
The Western Union man said, "Sir?"
held out an envelope,
a telegram.
Dad couldn't open it
for the trembling,
finally handed it to me.
Mom put her hands to her head
like she wasn't going to
listen.

I opened it, unfolded the square,
saw "War Department"
and read out loud.
"Deeply regret to inform you
your son 1st Lt Thomas G Carl
wounded December 15
Southwest Pacific Area.
Medical discharge,
letter to follow.
Ulio, the Adjutant General."
It took us a second
to understand.
Thomas was alive,
discharged.
He was coming home.
Mom sobbed.
Dad grabbed her in a hug,
wiping away tears.
"He's coming home, May."

September 1944
The Gophers

"That glass don't stop
them rascals,
we'll try something else."
Dad clapped a hand on
Charles Darney's shoulder
and we all stood looking out
over the graveyard.

Today we'd found the gopher tunnels
around Annylee's grave,
spiked them with glass from
Lurkey's plate window
after Bucky Barnes
put his dad's Chevrolet
through it.
Curtis Ray was there,
pulled me aside.
"So," he said,
"Tom's coming home."
I told him about it.
An official letter had arrived
a few days after the telegram,
and two days after that
a letter from Thomas himself.
"His jeep rolled," I said.
"Says he's got bandages
all the way up his arm.
Says he almost lost his head."
"Listen," he said. "Other night—
I didn't mean to be
a jerk."
"I know," I said,
"but you were."
"Yeah." He stubbed his boot at the
soft dirt.
"I'm gonna clean up my act," he said.
"I don't, the ace'll whip my ass.
Right?"
"Darn right," I said.

October 1944

The Surprise

I was clearing the table
after dinner
when we heard the car horns.
Sounded like more than one
and grew louder,
urgent.
"Somebody's on fire again," said Mom.
I went to the window
but couldn't see out
into the dark.
Dad went to the door,
opened it,
and Merle Stanton barged in,
Cyrus LeBeau behind him.
"Wyn! May!" Merle hailed us,
and Cyrus interrupted. "We got your boy!
Your boy's home!"
"I saw him in Canton," Merle wrapped up,
"getting off the bus."
"I saw him first!" put in Cyrus.
"Thought we should bring him on home."
I pushed through them.
There at the bottom of the steps
was Thomas,
tall and whole,
like a stranger,
waiting to be invited.
I launched myself from the steps,

ready to barrel into him
but stopped,
seeing the white bandages
at his neck
and up his arm.
"Hey, Bud." Thomas grinned,
and I laughed and hugged him,
careful.
When we stood apart,
I saw him double-take.
"Oh, boy—
I can't believe this!"
I grinned down at him.
It had finally happened:
I was taller by an inch.
Then Mom and Dad were there,
dragging us into the house
hugging, crying, kissing,
everyone talking at once.
Thomas showed us the bandages
and turned down his collar
to show the stitches
clear round the back of his neck.
"It's my hand that's not right.
They won't let me fly.
I'm home for good," he said,
sounding so downcast,
we felt bad for being happy.
Mom, after she recovered enough,
offered to make coffee
for Cyrus and Merle,

apologized for not having pie.
But they knew the party could wait,
and quick as they'd come,
they pumped Thomas's hand,
slapped his shoulder,
and left,
honking again
as their engines roared
and faded on down the hill,
leaving us to ourselves,
to our tears and wonder
that Thomas was alive, and well,
and home.

October 1944
Thomas

When Thomas was overseas,
we'd talk all the time
about him coming home.
"When Thomas gets back"—
we probably said that
six times a day.
Now he was home,
and it wasn't how I thought
it would be.
I don't mean he was
spooked
like some of the guys who'd fought
on the ground.

He was just different,
older, grown up.
We talked about Gabe,
walked together up the hill
to see the mound,
the new stone.
I left him there
and was almost done milking
before he came back
and grabbed a bucket
to help.
I wanted to ask him stuff,
about the flying, the bombing.
But he wasn't all that interested
in the war.
In Europe, we were winning:
the Allies had moved into Rome,
Paris.
In the Pacific, we'd finally taken Guam.
The papers talked
about moving in on Tokyo,
guessing any time now.
But Thomas wanted to talk about
college, about engineering,
building better planes.
That new G.I. Bill
meant the government would pay.
He talked about Pauline,
about settling down.
I told him about Grandpa and Grama.
About Jozef

and Stinky.
Not about Sarah.
One day, I was thinking how
after going off to war,
flying thousands of miles,
dropping bombs,
nearly getting killed,
what did Thomas want?
To go to school
and be with his girl.
And I thought
how weird that was.
Because in my own way,
that was pretty much
what I wanted, too.

October 1944
The Hat

In Canton
Stinky and I walked down Main Street,
him jabbering
and me looking for
Gumps' Dressmaking and Millinery.
I was fetching Mom's new hat,
but Dora Gump had moved.
Stinky was on about his scheme
for selling tools.
"They got piles of stuff—
saws, lanterns—all rusty,

just lyin' around."

Vine Street, Mom said,
then turn right.

"It's a gold mine!" he went on.

"So, how's that work?" I asked.

"You get it cheap from the farmer?"

"Heck," Stinky said,
"folks don't even know stuff's there,
just lyin' in the barn or wherever.
It's junk.
If I took it,
they'd never even notice."

We turned the corner at Vine—
and half a block ahead
was Sarah.

I hauled Stinky into a doorway.

"Shut up," I said.

I wanted to talk to Sarah,
but not with Stinky around.

I didn't want to see her at all
if I couldn't explain.

After a minute
I leaned out to look.

The coast was clear.

"I mean . . .
it ain't like stealing, right?"

Stinky started in again.

"I mean, the stuff's just
going to waste."

A few more yards
and we were at the shop.

"Sure, it's like stealing," I said,
pushing open the door
and making the bell jangle.
"You take something
that's not yours—what else
you gonna call it?"
Dora Gump came out of the back room.
"Hello, dear!" she said
in her fluttery way.
"You're here for your mother's hat,
and it's not ready.
I only need two minutes!
I don't suppose you'd wait?"
"Sure," I said. I didn't mind.
Here I was safe
from Sarah.
For some reason Stinky was quiet.
Dora reappeared with the hat and scissors.
"I just need to trim these threads."
She hesitated, looking around,
and before I could stop her,
she plopped the thing on my head
with a giggle.
"You make a fine hat stand—
hold still! Two more snips . . ."
And sure enough
it only took two snips
for Sarah to walk by
and look in the window.
I saw her glance in, double-take,
and stare.

Dora's daughter Shirlynn
was Sarah's best friend at school.
Sarah probably came by here
all the time.
I snatched the thing off my head.
"Just wrap it up," I grumbled,
watching Sarah push open the door,
getting ready to hear her
big laugh.
But she didn't laugh.
She didn't even come in,
just stuck her head in the door.
"Eddie," she said, "Jozef—
he's in jail.
They arrested him for setting that fire
at the Strothers'."
I stood there like an idiot,
not knowing what to say,
till Sarah looked disgusted.
"I thought you'd want to know,"
she finally said. "I thought maybe
you'd want to do something."
The door jangled shut
behind her.
When my brain started working again,
I turned to Stinky.
"They put him in jail!
What are we gonna do?"
"Eddie—" he replied,
backing toward the door, "I— I'm
feeling kinda sick.
I gotta go home."
And before I could ask what the matter was,

he was out the door.

October 1944
In Jail

The next day
I went to see Jozef.
At first Jerome wasn't going to let me in.
Desk sergeant,
too old and fat to patrol,
eating a cupcake,
licking crumbs out of the paper.
Sugar sprinkles in his mustache
moved up and down
when he talked.
"Are you a relative
of the incarcerated?" he asked.
"Come on, Jerome, you know I'm not.
I'm his friend."
"Hmmph," he said.
A sprinkle fell out of his mustache
onto the desk.
He wiped his face,
cleared his throat.
"Technically, visitation rights
are only to be extended
when the incarcerated . . ."
He kept looking at the side drawer
of his desk.
Probably another cupcake,

quite a treat,
what with the sugar ration.
"Oh, heck," he said,
"go on."
Jozef was sitting on a bench
behind the bars,
his clothes rumpled.
He looked old and tired.
He stood when he saw me.
"*Dzieki!* You are good—
you come to help."
"Jozef, I know you didn't do it, but—
I don't know how I can help."
He sat down again,
head in his hands.
I wished I knew what to do.
He shook his head. "I do no wrong."
He stood again and came to the bars.
"Eddie," he said quietly,
"in Nowy Targ,
prison . . . very bad.
Friends go there . . ."
He put his face in his hands.
"Jozef," I said,
"they won't hang you or anything!
You'll be safe in here."
He waited before speaking.
"Ya!" he said,
his voice harsh.
"Sheriff, he tell me I am safe here—
safe in the prison."

He looked at me.
"But he say maybe not safe
outside."

The Clue

Sunday after church
I went to the only person
who'd had the button:
Curtis Ray.
He opened the door,
surprised.
"What's up?" he asked.
"They arrested Jozef," I said,
"because of that button."
I hesitated. "Were—
were you the one that
found it?"
Curt got my point
but didn't get mad.
"Okay, you think
I stole it.
I don't blame you—
but I ain't no thief.
Lem found it
before I ever got there.
Said after they stopped farming
and Leo moved away
no one even went in that shed.

Weren't nothin' in it but
rusted-out tools."
I stared.
Old tools?
"Thanks, Curt. Sorry.
I had it all wrong."
I was at the bottom of the steps
when Curt hollered after me,
"Hey, Eddie!"
I stopped and turned.
"You think you're smart," he said,
"but you ain't always."
"What?" I asked.
"Your girl, Sarah?
She ain't with Reevy.
Never was.
You're a fool."
My face got hot.
"I know—" I said, shrugged,
cool,
and kept on walking
till I turned the corner and Curt couldn't see.
Then I jumped in the air
and ran.

October 1944
The Confession

At the Dawsons' place
Stinky's sisters washed diapers

on the porch.
In the kitchen Fern was up to her elbows
stirring soup, cutting biscuits,
the two littlest ones
whining.
"He's around somewhere,"
she said. "Tell him dinner's on soon."
I headed out to the yard
trailed by the triplets
and found him in the tractor shed.
"Jozef's in jail," I said,
"for starting that fire."
I never saw him look
so scared.
"Jeez, Eddie—oh, man."
He told the triplets to scram
and for once they did.
"I . . . I took the button.
I took it the day we was at the camp," he said,
looking down at the shears
he'd been sanding.
"He wasn't using it!
He was just keeping it,
for nothing.
I know it was wrong.
I guess it dropped outta my pocket
at the Strothers'."
That much was easy to believe.
"Stinky, did you set that fire?"
He looked about ready to cry.
"Eddie, I swear—

it was an accident.
You know I'd never do
nothin' like that on purpose.
I used to do chores there,
and I knew there was rusty junk.
So I went, and on the shelf
I seen these . . ."
Stinky paused,
looked down at his feet.
"Go on," I said.
"I seen these cigarettes."
He looked wretched,
like he thought he'd catch more hell
for smoking a cigarette
than for burning down
a house.
"There were matches,
and I just thought I'd try . . .
I was gonna see if I could blow smoke
out my ears.
But my fingers were froze
and the matches wouldn't catch, and
they dropped on the floor, and
I finally gave up and left,
only
I guess maybe one of them . . .
caught."
I shook my head.
"We gotta see the sheriff."
"I know," he said.
"Honest, Eddie, I was gettin' up nerve

to tell.
I didn't do it on purpose.
My folks are gonna kill me."
He sighed and put down
the shears.
"Okay," he said,
"let's go."

October 1944
The Right Thing

"Oh, my," Laura said
and sat right down
in the sheriff's own chair,
had to get a hankie out of her purse.
Lem put a hand on her shoulder,
and Dad got her some water.
Stinky's dad just stood there
looking miserable.
"Tell the rest," I prodded Stinky.
So he told how
he'd noticed the tools,
the old rakes and pulleys
and sheep shears
and knew Lem and Laura
would never know or care
if something disappeared
from all that mess.
He looked at me. "When I told you
about taking the tools,

I guess . . .
I guess I hoped you'd say
it didn't matter."
"And what about the silver?"
the sheriff asked.
"I had it a long time—but
I didn't sell it!
That's why I still had it.
I was gonna give it back," he said.
He turned to Jozef.
"Honest—I swear!
I was gonna tell.
I was gonna get you out."
Jozef nodded. "Yes,
I think is true.
Is good," he said.
Sheriff Graham stood up.
"Well, I'm satisfied."
He turned to Stinky's dad. "Dale,
I expect you feel like whalin' into
the boy,
but I'm gonna ask you to
work with me on this."
Dale looked grim, but nodded.
"Mirga, you can go.
You'll get your button back;
don't worry about that.
I'm sure as heck sorry.
Hope you understand."
Jozef looked about to reply,
but didn't.

I walked out with him.
"Things will be better now," I said.
"We see," he said
with a sigh.
I thought about Big Buss and the others,
and I understood:
why would things get better?
Nobody
would have believed Jozef
if Stinky hadn't told.

October 1944
The Talk

When Grama made muffins,
she always made
an extra dozen,
because that's how many
I could eat.
They were small,
and I was always hungry.
I was on about
the ninth one
before I finished telling her
about Jozef.
She was still on her second one,
sipping coffee.
"Well," she finally said,
"thing is, Big Buss and all—
they're cowards.

Like to talk big,
but they can't afford
to lose business.
Most folks around here
don't want trouble.
Seems that Mirga fellah
ain't a bad sort,
but others need to know it.
Maybe then Buss and them boys'd
think twice about
causing harm."
I reached for number ten,
thinking about that.
"I could talk to the sheriff," I said.
"Ask him to call on folks.
And maybe Reverend James
would say something
on Sunday.
And Dale and Lem
and Dad—
if I ask them,
they'll tell everyone how
Jozef does good shoeing."
Grama nodded.
I felt some better.
She started toward the sink
with the empty muffin tin,
stopped to put a hand
on my head.
"You know, Eddie,
you speaking up—"

her voice caught a little
"—you done good."

November 1944
The Apology

I'd been trying
to catch Sarah alone,
but she was always with Shirlynn
or other girls.
She didn't seem to notice
that I wasn't trying to ignore her
anymore.
Even if she did notice,
I wouldn't know what to say.
Stinky wasn't any help.
He was waiting
to see what the sheriff and his folks
were going to do.
The fire'd been an accident,
but there was still the stealing.
I think they were all worried
that any minute
he'd turn into some big criminal.
Anyway, he was grounded,
maybe forever.
After I made up my mind
to talk to Sarah
I spent a couple weeks thinking,
dreading,

imagining telling her
about everything.
I wanted her to know
about Jozef,
how things had changed.
I wanted to know
what she thought
about whether he'd be safe,
whether things would be
better.
Finally one day
leaving school
I hollered after her.
She waited while I caught up.
"Hey," I said,
"Sarah, I . . . well . . ."
She sure wasn't one
to beat around the bush.
"You want to apologize
for being stupid?" she said.
"Yeah."
"I did kiss him," she said.
I felt the knife in my heart—
maybe Curt was wrong.
She went on. "And if any other boy
I've known my whole life
wants a kiss for luck
the day he ships out,
he's gonna get it, too."
My face grew hot
and I had to look away

so I looked at my shoes.
"I'm sorry, Sarah.
Heck—
I'd enlist right now
if I thought I'd get a kiss
from you!"
If there was one thing I'd learned by then
it was that no one could predict
what Sarah would do,
so I stood there hopeful and
miserable
till she laughed and said,
"Easy for you to say—
you know you can't enlist!"
She handed me her books,
leaned a little closer.
"But maybe . . .
you won't have to."
My heart about left my body,
hearing her words.
Feeling the warmth
of that smile,
that smile from those lips,
Sarah's lips.
I put her books with mine
and shifted them to one side,
so I could put my arm around her
as we walked.